ART FROM SHELLS

a

b

c

d

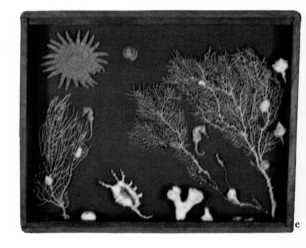

e

a A necklace made with an abalone shell and assorted hanging shells.

b A figurine that was described in Chapter 6.

c A scorpion conch on petrified wood.

d A coffee table housing part of our collection of shells.

e A soft coral and seahorse shadow box that was described in Chapter 6.

ART FROM SHELLS

by STUART AND LENI GOODMAN

**Jewelry•Sculptures•Collages
Figurines•Collections**

Crown Publishers, Inc.   New York

To Julie

∿∿

All photographs and designs are by the authors unless otherwise noted.

Inquiries should be addressed to Crown Publishers, Inc., 419 Park Avenue South, New York, N.Y. 10016.

Library of Congress Catalog Card Number: 72-84317
ISBN: 0-517-500248
ISBN: 0-517-500256

Printed in the United States of America
Published simultaneously in Canada by
General Publishing Company Limited

Design — Michael Perpich

ACKNOWLEDGMENTS

To Linda and Olga Oshrin, Knits Unlimited, New York, for their guidance and encouragement in helping us develop our shell jewelry. To Jerome M. Eisenberg, The Collector's Cabinet, New York, for the use of some of his shell designs and pictures in our book, and Barbra Sutton, noted conchologist, for her expert knowledge which she put at our disposal. And to Veronica Parker Johns, Seashells Unlimited, New York, our first contact with shell buying, for her lovely selection of shells which inspired some of our designs.

To Bill Slosky, Underwater Industries, St. Thomas, Virgin Islands, for sharing his knowledge of underwater photography with us. To Hana Motal of Motal Custom Darkrooms, New York, for her help and guidance in processing the photographs; and to Jules Germain, Brooklyn, New York, for his additional photographic help. To Susan Staff for modeling our jewelry and helping make the pieces come alive for the camera. To Gary Braunstein for helping arrange our initial contacts throughout the Philippines. To Jane Jordan of Hallmark Galleries, New York, who allowed us to photograph "The Collectors" display in the Gallery, and who wrote the paragraph that begins our chapter on shell collections.

To Mr. and Mrs. Wyatt Cooper (Gloria Vanderbilt) for permission to use the photographs of the lovely shell pieces that they collect. To Marion and Harry Zelenko for their permission to photograph their shell pieces. And to Rohm and Haas Company, for the pictures and information on Plexiglas. To Herbert Parker, D.D.S., for his help and expert tips on drilling the shells. To Mike Hart for her help in making the belts.

To Harriet and Joan Ellenbogen for their inspirational help and patience throughout it all. To Joan Cook of *The New York Times* for her initial interest in our shell creations as a newsworthy item, which brought us to the attention of Brandt Aymar, whose idea this book was.

And lastly to Brandt Aymar, our editor, for talking us into writing this book, which we have loved doing, and for his help and direction throughout.

CONTENTS

CONTENTS (continued)

FOREWORD

Today shell collecting is one of the fastest growing hobbies in the world. But it had its roots in ancient times. History tells many stories of the importance that shells played in everyday life in primitive times. Archaeologists have found cockleshells in tombs dating back to 2500 B.C. Shells, especially the money cowries, were used as a medium of exchange throughout the ancient world. In Africa, a wife could be bought for about 50,000 cowrie shells. As recently as the 1800s, trading nations imported money cowries for trading in Africa. And, of course, the American Indian used shell beads called "wampum" for currency. Throughout history, shells have been used as dishes, kettles, musical instruments, jewelry, and sacred objects. And the magnificent forms and shapes of shells have inspired architects and artists in their creative efforts. In this book we hope to share with you our love of shells, and inspire you in collecting and using your shells in a creative way. Although we do not attempt to be scientific or technical in our discussion of shells, we feel a basic knowledge of their origins and habitats is essential, and will help you in your quest for them. It will also enrich your enjoyment in collecting and using them in the art objects we will demonstrate to you, and in the further exploration that you will undoubtedly do on your own.

A bag of money cowries, the shells that were most commonly used as a medium of exchange from ancient times down through the 1800s.

ART FROM SHELLS

The World of Shells **1**

*F*rom the littlest toddler playing in the sand to the little old lady taking a walk on the beach, we all want to bring home a souvenir from the sea.

I remember as a child picking up shells at the beach, taking them home, playing with them, and then eventually relegating them to the junk drawer with the baseball cards and old marbles. But strangely enough, years later when the marbles were lost and the baseball cards were traded away, the seashells remained as beautiful as when they were first found.

In this chapter we will explain where and how the many species of shells live and the many ways to obtain them around the world.

First, to help you understand and appreciate shells even more than you probably already do, we would like to give you a brief definition of what a shell is.

Zoologically, shells are classified as phylum Mollusca. Thus we get the word *mollusk*. The shell itself is the external skeleton of an animal without a backbone, an invertebrate.

The soft body of most mollusks is protected by a hard covering, which we know as the "shell." This shell is a calcareous covering made by a secretion through a modified part of the body wall of the mollusk, called the mantle. Over a period of weeks, this secretion becomes hard and eventually forms the protective covering for the mollusk.

As you know all shells are not alike. Some are brightly colored, some are drab, some are knobbled, and some are smooth.
Top row: Murex nigritus, turban shell, ram's murex.
Bottom row: Tiger cowrie, egg shell, lettered cone.

There are reasons for these differences. Inside the mollusk there are certain parts of the mantle that are responsible for different aspects of the shell. Some parts form the sculpturing of the shell, some form the ridges, the knobs, the spines, the unique color patterns. And some parts form the outer coat (periostracum), which makes the shell smooth, or gives it a coat of fur, or even a fiberlike covering.

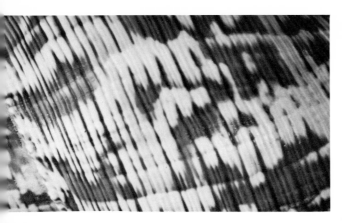

Two different patterns.

The first pattern as you can see is from a tulip shell.

The other pattern as you can see is from a map cowrie.

Classes of Shells

Some mollusks such as the octopus and sea slugs have no shells, while others have an internal one, as in the cases of the squid and cuttlefish.

Most of the shells found by collectors are broken down into two of the six classes or major divisions of mollusks.

The univalves ("stomach-footed" gastropods) are snails, whose single shell is usually in a spiral shape. There are 80,000 gastropod species known. Half of these inhabit salt water, the other half are freshwater or land species.

Most of these snails, which include conchs, cones, cowries, olives, top shells, and more, move from place to place by crawling along on a muscular padlike foot. Most species have a horny or calcareous plate attached to their foot (the operculum), which is used to protect the soft part of the mollusk when it withdraws into its shell. However, there are many predators that are treated to a delicious meal, for this "trap door" doesn't always close tightly.

A helmet shell walking along the bottom with its padlike foot.

The bivalves (hatchet-footed pelecypods) need no operculum to protect them from predators. They have a pair of hinged shells, or valves, that close. Like snails they also have a foot to move along with, but theirs is more wedgelike and not as large. Thus they don't move as quickly. However, some of them can leap or burrow with a great deal of agility. Some can even bore into wood or rocks. These bivalves are also a great food source. For those of you who haven't had oysters Rockefeller or clams casino or a mussel stew, you are in for a delicacy.

A group of bivalves.
Top row: Ark shell (or turkey wing), rock oyster, bear paw clam, *Pecten swifti.*
Center row: Atlantic Bay scallop, king venus, lucine clam, sunrise tellin.
Bottom row: Razor clam (or jackknife clam).

The other four classes of mollusks are:
1. The scaphopods, or tusk shells. They resemble the tusks of elephants, only much smaller. There are about two hundred of these species known.

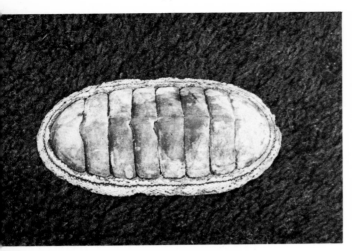

2. The Amphineura, or chitons, are in a class by themselves. If found on a beach they might resemble a limpet (which is a gastropod), but don't be mistaken. They are quite distinguishable by their eight-plated coat of armor. They usually attach themselves to rocks by the water's edge, and have such an adherent quality that you would need a heavy knife or abalone bar to free them. There are about six hundred shallow-water species known.

3. The cephalopods are the most highly developed of all mollusks. They are called the "head-footed" mollusks. They have very strong jaws and large eyes, probably because they prefer the darkness. They are often found in caves or under rocks and coral. There are about eight hundred species of these, which Jules Verne fantasized as sea monsters: octopus, squid, cuttlefish, as well as the chambered nautilus, and the fragile paper nautilus (argonaut). Except for the giant squid, all are not much more than a few feet across from tentacle to tentacle, and really quite passive (contrary to all those underwater movies one sees).

The chambered nautilus, from which are cut the beautiful pearlized drops called "tiger's eyes."

4. And last is a limpetlike species known until recently only from fossils called Monoplacophora. It is a rare deep-sea species.

The malacologists of today are still probing the inner depths of our oceans and probably in the near future will discover more classes of phylum Mollusca.

The Provinces

The world of shells is divided into provinces much the same way our continents, countries, states, cities, and towns are divided.

We will list the different provinces and describe some of the shells you might find in each of these provinces.

The dividing lines between these provinces are not exact. Different currents, storms at sea, and other phenomena can carry shells from one province to another. So if you are collecting shells in San Diego, California, for example, it is possible that you might find a tent olive from the Panamic Province.

First, in North America there is the *Californian Province,* which stretches from the state of Washington to Lower California. There are about 2,100 species of shells in this province, including the abalones (which we use in many of our jewelry pieces), murex rock shells, limpets, large chitons, and purple dwarf olive shells.

To the north of the Californian Province are the icy waters of the *Aleutian Province.* Since most mollusks prefer more temperate waters, there are not many species that live in this province. Some species of scallops, the leafy Purpura, and clams are native to it. There are so few species in this province that many books on shells don't even list it.

On the East Coast, first comes the *Boreal Province,* which extends from Maine to Labrador. This also is very cold water and not a haven for shell fauna. Some clams and snails are native to this province.

Next comes the *Carolinian Province,* where most of us in the eastern United States will do our collecting. It stretches from Cape Cod, Massachusetts, to the northern part of Florida and then westward into Texas. It does not include the southern tip of Florida (which lies in the tropical Caribbean Province). Shark-eye moon shells, quahog clams, oyster drill shells, marsh periwinkles, and the New England neptune are just some of the species found in this province.

The *Caribbean Province* is just where it says. It is centered in the heart of the West Indies, but stretches its arm north to the southern tip of Florida and Bermuda. Many species in this province will be found southward as far as South America. The beautiful queen conch is characteristic of this province. There are about 1,200 species here, including the sunrise tellin, bleeding tooth, tulip shell, bubble shell, conchs (Florida fighting conchs, milk conchs, hawk-wing conchs, etc.), West Indian top shells, and West Indian turkey wings.

From the Gulf of California to northern Ecuador is the *Panamic Province.* In earliest geologic times this area was connected with the Caribbean, which accounts for much of the similar fauna. The *Murex nigritus* (which we use in our sculptures) is native to this province, as are the colorful tent olives, grinning tuns, and strombina whelks. There is talk nowadays of a new Panama Canal that would link the Pacific and Caribbean waters and perhaps open a whole new oceanographic study.

The largest shell region is the *Indo-Pacific Province.* It extends from East Africa eastward through the East Indies to Polynesia. This province is so large that it is divided into subregions.

The Red Sea is one of these regions. It lies in a pocket of the Indian Ocean. Many unique species can be found here, such as the lineated conch and the thrush cowrie.

Australia, with its Great Barrier Reef, has many rare and colorful shells. Volutes, cones, cowries, and large tritons are familiar to this area. These tritons are becoming scarce, though. Since the problem with the increasing amount of "crown of thorn" starfish, which eat away and destroy the coral reefs, the Australian government may forbid you to take a triton from their waters (although the situation has recently begun to improve). Many scientists believe that the triton feeds upon these starfish.

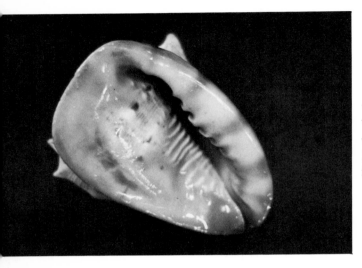

The Indo-Pacific helmet shell. Whereas the triton will eat starfish when nothing else is available, the Indo-Pacific helmet shell's main diet is starfish and sea urchins.

The Hawaiian chain lacks many of the normal Indo-Pacific species; however, it does have many smaller conchs (Diana conch, dog conch, black mouth conch, etc.), and cones and cowries, and some beautiful auger shells.

Cone shells from the Indo-Pacific Province.

The Philippines, which are spread out and consist of thousands of little islands, are probably the world's largest suppliers of shells. Thousands of different species live in their many tropical waters and coral gardens. Everything from the tapestry turban to the giant *Tridacna* to the famed glory-of-the-sea has been found here.

The giant *Tridacna*. Many people use this magnificent large shell as a showpiece in their homes.

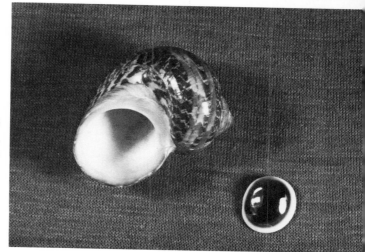

The tapestry turban shell and its operculum, the "cat's eye," which can be used in making beautiful cufflinks and rings.

Years ago many pearl oysters were found in Polynesia and the Philippine area. However, today many of your pearls are raised in underwater colonies in the *Japanese Province*. It lies between the Aleutian and the Indo-Pacific provinces. The central islands of Japan house many species of shell fauna. The emperor's slit shell, which is a collector's delight, is found in this province, along with species of cones, whelks, murex, and volutes. Many colorful scallops can also be found in the Japanese Province.

The emperor's slit shell from the Japanese Province.

The *South African Province* has about nine hundred species of shells as unique as the dense jungles of its mainland. Unusual limpets, large clams and cockleshells, the Prometheus cone (the largest living cone shell), and multicolored cowries are found in its cool waters. Diving for live shells here is difficult because of the rough waters. But the beachcombing is fantastic, as many beautiful and perfect specimens are thrown up on the shore by these same rough waters.

And last, one of the world's historic seas makes up one of the richest areas for shell fauna. The *Mediterranean Province* (also known as the *Lusitanian Province*) stretches from Portugal to Southern France to the northern coast of Africa. It has about 1,400 species of mollusks. The Shell Oil Company uses a common shell of this area as its trademark, the Jacob's scallop. Lurid cowries, spiny helmets, and pelican's foot shells are some mollusks often found in this province.

The purple dye murex from the Mediterranean Province was used as a source of dye in the days of the Phoenicians.

Along with the knowledge of the provinces it would be helpful to know the four worlds where marine mollusks live.

The pelagic world houses mollusks near the surface of the oceans. Some float, some attach themselves to seaweed, others just hover in mid-water. The purple sailor is one example.

The littoral world supports thousands of shell fauna along miles of shoreline. Some live between high and low tide. Such shells as the periwinkle, limpet, clam, and slipper shells can be found in this world.

The shallow-water world contains most of the world's mollusks. This shallow-water world stretches down to a depth of about four hundred feet. Almost every species of shell can be found here.

The abyssal world has almost no light and stretches down miles to the inner depths of the ocean floor. The water temperature is near freezing and produces a nearly colorless, small species of shells. All abyssal world species of shells are similar, no matter what province they come from. Some species that live in this world are latiaxis shells and turrids. There is much to be learned from this world, and probably thousands of species of shells yet to be discovered and named.

Finding Shells

DIVING

The most rewarding way of obtaining shells is to dive for them, as finding shells in their natural habitat yields the most perfect shell.

Stuart Goodman using scuba gear which is a self-contained underwater breathing apparatus consisting of an underwater tank, regulator, fins, mask.

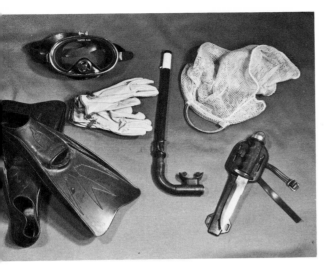

Skin-diving gear consists of fins, mask, and snorkle. Also included here are a net, gloves, and a knife, all of which will help you gather shells underwater.

A word of caution in regard to diving equipment. Scuba gear is widely available for rent. But you should not attempt to use it without a physical check-up and instruction from a NAUI (National Association of Underwater Instructors) or other qualified teacher. Even in just snorkling, one should have some formal instruction.

Now that you are ready for your descent into the "silent world" outfitted like Lloyd Bridges, don't be too disappointed if you don't get any shells on your first few dives. In fact, without some knowledge of where to look and what to look for, you might not even see any shells.

Each of the shell species lives in different places under the water. We will show you some of the species and explain where they live and how to collect them most easily.

Probably the easiest shell to find underwater in the Caribbean or Florida area is the conch.

A variety of conch shells from the Caribbean Province.

Can you find the conch shell crawling along the sandy bottom?

They are the most common and make a beautiful shell for a sculpture. To find a conch, look for a trail in the sandy bottom. As we explained before, the conch, a stomach-footed gastropod, crawls along the bottom by extending his foot and pulling his shell after him. Follow this trail and you will find your conch. Just pick him up and put him in your "goodie bag," a net bag used for collecting and carrying shells. Or you can use a lingerie laundry bag.

There are many gastropods that crawl along in exactly the same way as the conch. Here is a Florida horse conch shell pulling itself along. The shank shell, the tulip, the helmet, the triton, and the cone shell all behave in a similar manner.

The auger and the olive species also leave a slight trail in the sand. Some of them might be buried in the sand at the end of their trail.

A variety of olive shells.

As many of these species also feed on grassy bottoms, there might not be a trail to follow. However, if you familiarize yourself with their shapes, you might be able to spot them among the seaweed or eelgrass.

Sometimes you might think you are hot on the trail of a shell and wind up with a horseshoe crab instead. But that is all part of the fun.

We should at this point mention "hermit crabs." They are soft crabs, without a hard shell covering of their own, that seek out empty or dead shells as their home. As they grow larger, they discard their present home and seek a larger one. Many perfect and beautiful shells are used as homes by these crabs. So if you are following a trail in the sand and see a shell scooting away from you rather quickly, it is probably a hermit crab.

The top shells (trochus family) are also very easy to find. They cling to rocks and coral and look like a child's top.

The West Indian top shells are black and white or brown and white. The Pacific top shells are more brightly colored in greens and reds.

These shells as well as some of the others might not be as distinguishable underwater, because they are sometimes covered with coral or blend into the rock or coral they cling to. Or some shells will be buried or partially buried under some sand.

Try to learn the shells by species and by sizes and shapes. Different shell species grow to different sizes, although obviously they do maintain their basic family shape.

Cowries.

The cowrie shell, which is probably the most sought after and variously colored of the mollusks, is also the hardest to find. It lives on and under dead coral and rocks in the water, and only comes out at night to feed. We find the best way to get these shells is to turn over small rocks and dead corals and look under them. Usually the cowrie will cling to the underside, and all you have to do is pick it off and put it in your goodie bag. Usually these pieces of dead coral and rocks are found near the bases of large coral heads and in cavelike holes in these coral formations. But before reaching for them be sure they are not sharing their home with a moray eel. If you turn the rocks and coral pieces back over again after removing the cowries you will be helping future mollusks find a home to cling to.

A good practice in diving for shells is to always use caution. Look before you leap. As beautiful as the underwater world is, there are some predators that could be harmful if disturbed. Not to mention sharks and barracuda (although we have dived in schools of barracudas without incident, and there are no known fatalities from them).

A shell collector in diving must be on the alert against the following potential dangers:

Sea urchins, which if stepped on or brushed against can inflict a painful barb.

Stonefish and lion-fish, which have poisonous barbs that extend from their bodies.

Fire coral and other sharp coral. Fire coral produces a burn, as its name would suggest. The other coral can scratch and cause infection as it contains many bacteria. Pictured is a type of elkhorn coral.

Moray eels, who might be inhabiting a deep hole or dark cave you decide to probe into. One good thing about them is that they usually will only attack to protect their home.

Sea anemone. They are beautiful and varicolored and seem to flow back and forth like a flower blowing in the wind. The beautiful wentletrap shell lives in and at the root of the sea anemone, feeding off its catch, much like a parasite. Be careful in collecting the wentletrap for most sea anemones have a stinging power that can be extremely harmful to some people. Use a knife to free the shell.

It is a good idea to wear gloves while diving and collecting to avoid dangers from the above. We find that leather workgloves are excellent for this purpose. They are available in most hardware stores for under two dollars. Of course, diving shops have more expensive gloves for this purpose as well.

The marble cone, one of the venomous cones of the Indo-Pacific.

The cone family of shells is also desirable for collecting because of their beautiful colors and interesting shape. Some varieties are quite rare. They are shaped like an ice cream cone, hence their name. They crawl along the sandy bottom and leave a trail for you to follow. However, some of the Pacific and Indian Ocean cones have a poisonous barb (proboscis) that can be harmful and even fatal, as it paralyzes the nervous system. So if you are diving in these waters, learn to recognize these cones and pick them up only with a small strainer. Touch them only at the fat or top end of the conical, as the barb juts out from the thin spiraled end.

In spite of the danger involved, these cone shells are beautiful and worth the extra caution.

BIVALVES These shells are found buried under the sand in the water, or sometimes just sitting on the bottom. Sometimes there is a hole in the top of a sand mound and all you have to do is dig a few inches with your hands or knife and you have your treasure. Some bivalves will extend above the sand. Others might have a long thin siphon sticking out of the sand.

This family of shells also lives under the sand out of the water. So look for holes in the sand near the water's edge while strolling down the beach.

This is a rough file clam. It loses its hairy fibers when it dies.

A lot of areas where you dive might not have a coral garden or rocks or a sandy bottom. Instead there will be a grassy bottom. This is called eelgrass or seaweed or kelp. Don't pass it up, because many shell species live in this grass.

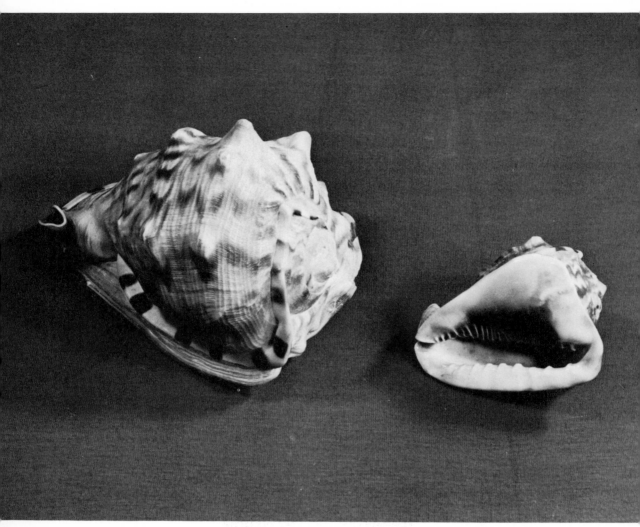

The helmet shell from which cameos are carved lives in this type of area.

The tulip and pen shells also live in this eelgrass.

The pen shell, however, will not be walking along the bottom as the helmet and tulip shells will do. Rather it will be almost completely buried in the sandy clearing between the eelgrass, with just the top ridge above the sand. Just pull firmly and the pen shell will come free. However be careful, as it is quite fragile and might break. The meat inside is similar to mussel or clam meat and is quite delicious raw.

Starfish are also quite abundant in eel-grass and seaweed. They are brightly colored orange or deep red when alive. After being exposed to the air and sun they become beige or brown.

We will never forget an afternoon in the Bahamas, on Great Exuma Island, where we met a native who took us to a sandbank covered with eelgrass. It was nearly low tide and we spent a fantastic afternoon walking over the bar in sneakers and finding more helmet shells, tulip shells, and giant orange starfish than one could possibly ever carry back. We took a few helmet and tulip shells as our momentos and left the rest to nature.

There are, of course, many more species of shells, some of which we will dis-cuss in beachcombing. The only other shell we would like to mention here is the flamingo tongue shell. It lives and feeds on sea fans particularly the gorgonian which is a form of soft coral. We point this out to make you aware of the variety of places one can find mollusks underwater.

The flamingo tongue is a beautiful orange-colored shell.

But when it is clinging to the gorgonian (pictured) or sea fan, it covers this orange shell with its fleshy spotted mantle. When it is touched it will withdraw this mantle, thus showing its orange shell. Some other shells, such as some of the volutes, will also do the same thing.

There are many predators of the mollusk. Probably the greatest predator is other mollusks which are carnivorous. They will attack those shells that feed off algae and plankton. Also larger mollusks will often attack smaller species. The tulip shell eats conchs, the starfish eats all shells, and as we mentioned earlier the triton and the Indo-Pacific helmet shell feed upon starfish.

Crabs are a great threat to the mollusk. I can remember fighting a crab for a beautiful scotch bonnet shell it had in its claws. I finally won but the crab did chip the shell.

A starfish caught in the act of eating a mussel.

Lobster and shrimp are also great enemies of the mollusk.

However, in this growing business of obtaining shells by collectors, jewelry and button manufacturers throughout the world, and those seeking a source of food, the mollusk has acquired a new predator—man.

In the Philippines the shell industry is one of the islands' largest industries, employing thousands of people. In Mexico it has become so large that the government has taken over control of it.

Although there are billions of shells throughout the world, we should be aware what this growing activity can mean in the near future in relation to the shell. We must do everything in our power to allow mollusks to live and continue to multiply.

There are already many national underwater parks and gardens where the shell is protected from man's quest for it. We can help by taking only those shells we actually need in our collecting and creative endeavors.

DREDGING

This is also an excellent way to get the best specimens of shells. But the kinds of shells you can get are limited, because you can dredge only over a sandy or grassy bottom; you obviously can't get the shells that cling to rocks or coral or that are buried too deeply in the sand.

You can dredge from any size boat as long as it is powered by an outboard motor. A funnel-like attachment, made up of wooden planks, scrapes the bottom of the area and funnels what is picked up into a net at the end.

Pick a small area to dredge and work back and forth like a lawn mower, so that you will be able to recover any shells that spill out. Move very slowly through the water. After some practice this should yield a fine harvest of shells.

When you haul in the net, it is a rather messy job. We suggest you wear a rubber apron and gloves. The net will probably be heavy, and you will need two people to lift it into the boat.

You can buy a commercial net or make your own. It is similar to a lobster net, but is more tightly woven and has a stiff rod at the bottom.

BEACHCOMBING

Probably the easiest way to get shells is by strolling along the beach and just picking them up. Although they won't be in the best condition, some of them will be usable and beautiful enough to use in making art objects and jewelry. And occasionally you will find some perfect specimens that have recently been washed up onto the beach especially after a big storm.

A great many shells can be found at the water's edge, or in a few inches of water. To find bivalves, look for air holes in the wet sand or mud if it is a bay. This is one of the traces the shell leaves.

Notice how some of these coquina (butterfly shells) are burrowing their way into the sand.

Watch the seagulls and you will usually find shells near them, as they sometimes eat fresh mollusks that have been washed ashore.

Some holes will contain crabs instead of shells, but these are fun to find as well.

Sometimes tiny starfish are found on wet sand. As we mentioned earlier, larger starfish are found in eelgrass on sandbars. At low tide, just walk onto the sandbar and pick them up.

While walking along the beach you usually come to some large rocks or coral heads protruding from the water. You might think to just walk around them— but a shell collector won't. He walks down to the water's edge by the rocks, and discovers colored nerites, bleeding tooth shells, and chitons attached to the rocks. These shells make their homes in potholes on these rocks and coral heads, which jut out above the water. They cling to the rock, and some of them walk around little pockets in the rocks and coral. Just pick them off and put them in your bag. The chitons probably need to be pried off with a knife or abalone bar, as they cling like a rubber suction pad. You might also find top shells out of water this way.

Also look for patches of seaweed along the beach and examine them closely. There are some shells that live in the roots and feed off this weed. You might find some perfect specimens this way.

If the beach you are walking along happens to be in Florida, be careful of Portuguese man-of-war, which when washed ashore looks like a blue bubble. Don't step on it or try to break the bubble, for even when dead this sea creature (a member of the jellyfish family) can inflict a nasty sting. Some of the larger ones can be fatal to those people who are allergic to its sting, as some people are allergic to bee stings.

The reason we mention the Portuguese man-of-war is that a beautiful shell called the purple sailor (*Janthina janthina*) sometimes travels with it. These shells are often washed ashore with the man-of-war. Take care when removing the shells not to burst the bubble. Probably the best way is to push the shell away from it with a stick and then pick the shell up.

After you have combed your beach and collected as many shells as you want for your jewelry and art objects, your interest might be diverted to the smooth stones and sea glass that you see on the beach.

These stones and pieces of glass, which have been polished to perfection by the pounding surf, can be used in making sea collages and jewelry, or paperweights and other decorative objects. You might also find a beautifully colored glass ball or two on the beach. These are used in fishing nets and sometimes float ashore.

Many people don't realize that the ocean is not the only place that mollusks live. There are also freshwater snails and bivalves that breed and live in lakes and rivers.

There are also some shells that live on trees. The periwinkle is a sea snail that spends much of its time out of water. It is found on the trunks and limbs of mangroves by saltwater inlets in Florida and the West Indies. To survive it needs just the salt air and the little water it gets during high tide.

There are other tree snails, some of which are shaped like bullets and can be picked off trees along the beach. Enough of them can make a beautiful bracelet.

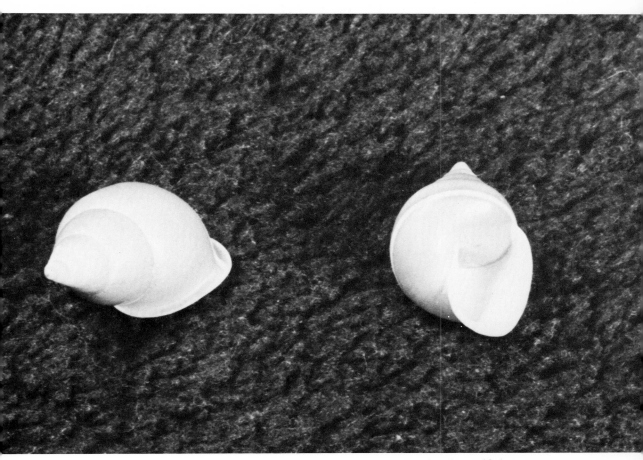

An example is the beautiful green tree snail of Africa, which is probably the most sought after of the tree snails. Its size and color make it very useful in jewelry design for earrings and brooches.

We have just touched upon the basic species of shells to familiarize you enough to begin collecting shells for art and jewelry making. Remember, keep your eyes open and you will come home with a goodie bag full of fascinating objects from your day of beachcombing.

BUYING SHELLS

If you live in an area that is nowhere near a beach or lake, and your vacation time is a long way off, your shells are probably as close as your Yellow Pages. (Also see our Index of Supplies for shell sources.) You can order shells directly from these sources just by specifying type and size, after receiving their catalogues or list of shells and prices.

Many collectors and hobbyists often buy their shells. One advantage is that your shells will already be cleaned and sometimes polished, and thus ready to use immediately.

In the beginning, when we started making our shell jewelry, we used only the shells we dove for and picked up ourselves. Even now we display in our home only the shells we actually found ourselves. I guess we consider it a point of honor. But once we started selling the jewelry and art objects we made, our supply was insufficient for our growing business. And the time it took to clean the shells! It soon was necessary for us to find sources to buy shells.

We found to our pleasant surprise that these sources had such beautiful selections, and much more varied assortments than we had, that we were intrigued all over again with the diversity of nature and the wonder of the shell. And this diversified selection certainly added to the beauty of our jewelry. Not only the diversity of types of shells but the diversity of colors that comes from the different provinces of the world is breathtaking.

So, by all means, don't hesitate to explore the whole area of browsing and buying shells.

In summary, we would say, whether you dive for your shells, find them as you go strolling along a beach, or buy them from a store, you will enjoy the experience and the beauty of the shells, and you will be able to discover the joy and satisfaction from creating your own works of art from these natural works of art.

Cleaning and Preparation of Shells **2**

Materials and Tools

*H*ere are some of the materials needed to clean your shells and prepare them for use.

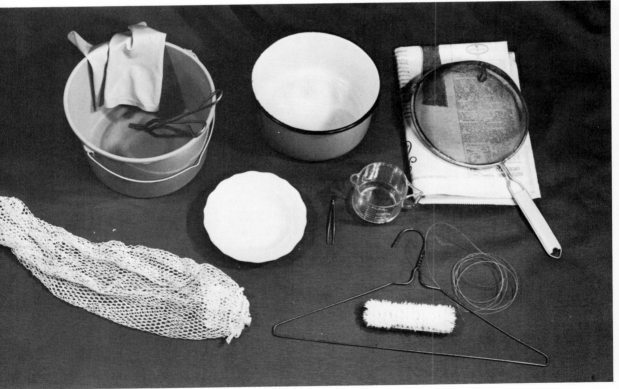

Pictured are the goodie bag, a large bucket (or two), rubber gloves, tongs, a scrub brush, a wire hanger to use as hook, nylon fishing line, measuring cup, tweezers, a small bowl, a pot for boiling, a strainer, and, of course, newspapers.

Also needed are: Clorox, muriatic acid (available from a hardware store), alcohol, mineral oil, lighter fluid, Krylon Crystal Clear acrylic spray (optional), and toweling or rags.

Techniques of Cleaning

Now that you have had the pleasure of diving and beachcombing for your treasures, here comes the work.

You are probably wondering how to get that terrible smell out of your shells, and also how to make them as bright and clean as the shells you have seen in collections or in this book. If you have kept your treasures around for a few days you know what we mean by the smell. There is nothing worse than the smell of a decaying sea animal inside a shell.

There is a certain customs official at Kennedy Airport who will never forget that smell. We were on our way back from a diving trip in the Caribbean, with a canvas bag filled with shells several days old with the animals still inside. We had not been able to extract them as we had had very limited facilities in our hotel room. Well, this gentleman asked us to open our luggage for inspection, and unfortunately he pointed to the canvas bag first. As we started to unzip it, the odor of dead fish began to fill the air. "My God, what is that terrible smell?" he asked. We tried to open the bag further as we explained about our shells, but he had had enough. He quickly waved us through and out of customs without a second glance at any of our other luggage.

In this chapter we will discuss the various ways of overcoming the problem—that is, how to clean your shells of their animal life and how to rid them of that stale ocean smell that often accompanies them. Then we will show you how to brighten your shells and bring out their hidden colors, so that they will be ready to use in making shell jewelry and art objects.

HANGING

Hanging might seem like a strange way to rid the shell of its animal, and at first we didn't believe how well it could work. It is not the easiest method, but if you are away from home and haven't any of the other methods available to you, you had better know about hanging.

Hanging works best for the larger shells you might find, as the principle is that the weight of the shell does the work for you. (This process is not to be used with the dangerous cone shells from the Pacific, discussed in Chapter 1.)

First, you need a piece of string or nylon fishing line. Make a slip knot at one end. As soon as you find the shell and the animal is still alive, place it in the sun. In a few minutes the animal will begin to come out of his shell in order to pull himself away from the hot sun. As he comes out, gently slip the string around his foot (operculum) and pull tightly. He will immediately try to go back into his shell house, but if the string is tightly tied, he will be caught.

Then tie the other end of the string onto a branch or a hanging ledge a few feet off the ground until the weight of the shell forces it to fall off, leaving the animal tied to the end of the string.

This process takes a few hours as the muscles that keep the animal attached to the shell gradually loosen and finally let go. An advantage to this method is that you usually get the complete animal out in one piece without the problem of the tip breaking off and remaining inside the coils of the shell to rot and smell.

As the shell falls three or four feet in the process, make sure that the area below is cushioned in some way, so that the shell is not damaged when it drops.

If you are a fisherman, the animal can be used for bait. If you are a gourmet, and the shell you have hung up is a conch, the foot, when cleaned and pounded to make it tender, makes a delicious chowder, stew, or salad. Some people marinate the meat for steaks, but it is a bit tough. The taste is similar to the abalone, which is very popular on the West Coast. Conch meat is a very popular dish throughout the Caribbean.

ALCOHOL

The best way to clean out the tiny shells, such as periwinkles, cowries, olives, very small cones, or any very small species of gastropods, is by placing them in a solution of 80 percent alcohol and 20 percent water.

Then pull out the tiny animal with a pin or tweezers.

BOILING

Another method of cleaning the shell is by boiling it. This method is necessary for shells that are too small or difficult to hang.

As in the hanging method, it is best to boil the shell when the animal is still alive. This may sound cruel, but remember once the shell is out of water for any length of time, the animal will surely die anyway.

Let us emphasize, *don't* try to pick the animal out of the shell before you boil it, as you will break off part of it and make it much more difficult, if not impossible, to pull the remainder out after the boiling.

Larger shells should be dropped in boiling water for 10 to 15 minutes, and smaller shells up to 3 or 4 inches, no more than 5 minutes. Use an old pot and put the shells in a net bag (laundry lingerie bag, or the "goodie bag" you used in collecting them). This prevents the shells from banging around in the pot while they are boiling, and thus chipping or breaking.

When your shells are finished, remove them to an old dish or container, and place them under cold water to cool off. Then gently (with tweezers, or a hook or wire hanger for the larger shells), pull the animal slowly out of its shell. If you are not squeamish, you can get a good grip on the foot (operculum) with your hand, and thus slide the animal out of the larger shells in this manner. You know you have the entire animal out if the tip comes to a point.

Using a stiff vegetable brush, scrub the outer surfaces of the shells to remove any foreign matter that still clings.

Boiling is fast and not too involved, and usually works very well. However, there is one drawback. The boiling might take some of the natural colors out of the shells. We found that about half the shells do lose some of the beautiful colors they previously had.

FREEZING

Freezing is the best method for removing the animal from its shell, because, although it takes the longest, the shell does not lose any of its natural colors, and there is no chance of chipping or breaking. As in the other methods, the sooner you can freeze the shell the easier the removal will be.

Place the shell or shells in waxed paper and leave in the freezer for at least twelve hours. The animal must be completely frozen for this method to work.

Then place the shell in a pot of lukewarm water to thaw out, for about an hour. Remove the animal with tweezers, hook, or your hands, as suggested in the section on boiling.

OTHER METHODS

It is very easy to clean the bivalves (pelecypods). Just drop them in a bucket of fresh water for thirty minutes.

Pry them open.

Scrape out the insides with a knife. Then scrub the remainder out with a toothbrush or stiff vegetable brush.

There are other methods of getting the animals from their shells. However, we don't recommend them as they are too time-consuming and frustrating. And after all, you do want to start using your shells in art objects and jewelry as soon as possible.

One of these methods is to bury the shell in the sand (or dirt) and let the crabs or ants eat out the animal. This takes up to two weeks depending on the size of the shell and how hungry the crabs or ants are.

After the animal is removed from its shell using whichever method you find best, wash the shell out and let it dry in the sun or on some newspapers. Now your shells are ready for the last few steps that will bring out the luster and true colors of the shells.

Finishing and Polishing

CLOROX

The Clorox method is best used for all shells; however, it is essential for cowries and olives (as these shells should not be submerged in muretic acid).

Simply pour about a cup of Clorox bleach into two quarts of water. Add the shells and let them soak for a few hours. Then rinse them off and let them dry on some newspapers.

Clorox is essential in cleaning coral, to get rid of the odor and to obtain the whitest color possible. First wash the coral with a strong stream of water, from a hose or at full pressure in the sink. This will clear out most of the animal and some of the color. Then soak the coral in a strong Clorox solution (one cup of Clorox to three cups of water) overnight. Then dry out in the air. This of course is not to be used with black or red coral which maintains its color.

MURIATIC ACID *

As we mentioned, this method should not be used on any shell that has a hard shiny surface that looks naturally polished such as the cowries or olive. The acid would eat away the natural shiny surface and thus spoil the appearance of the shell.

But on shells without this shiny finish, the muretic acid works wonders by removing the top layer of foreign material that has accumulated on the shell. The natural colors of the shell are, in fact, highlighted by this process.

First a word of caution. Muriatic acid is dangerous to work with. Follow the directions on the label very carefully, and be sure to have proper ventilation when using it. Be careful not to let it come in contact with your skin, as this acid will eat it away to the bone. Always use rubber gloves while working with it.

Muriatic acid may be purchased in a hardware store in quart or half-gallon containers. Use a hard plastic or glass bucket to pour the acid into. Mix a cup of acid to every three cups of water. If you have a large amount of shells you'll probably have to double the amount to cover the shells.

Use a medium-size strainer to hold the shells while submerging in the solution. For very large shells you can use a pair of kitchen tongs.

Now that we have stressed the hazards of working with this acid, let us stress the wonders it can work on your shells.

Here is an abalone shell before its muriatic acid treatment.

* Most conchologists would not approve of using muriatic acid as they feel it takes away the natural look of the shell. However here we are concerned with making the natural shell as vibrant as possible for use in objects of art and recommend its use for this purpose only.

The acid will bubble as the shell is lowered into it.

Here is that same shell 10 seconds later.

An average shell that is not too badly encrusted with coral should take from 5 to 10 seconds to clean. Work upwards from that figure depending on how badly the shell is encrusted and how thick it is. If you leave a shell submerged too long, you will find part of your shell eaten away, as you see here with this donkey's ear.

A badly encrusted shell may take 30 seconds to a minute at the most, and usually less. Watch the shells closely and keep pulling them out to check on their progress, or you might wind up with an empty sieve. After a few mishaps you will get a feeling of the proper timing. Remember these timings are based on a 1 to 3 ratio. The stronger the solution the less time it takes.

It's a good idea to have a bowl or pail with water running into it, in the sink next to you. When you take the shells out of the muriatic acid solution, let the water run over them and drop them into the pail to rinse off. Then pull them out after a few minutes to dry on newspaper.

POLISHING AND SHINING

After you have cleaned your shells fully you might want to give them a bit more luster.

We mix three parts lighter fluid with one part clear mineral oil, and lightly coat the shells. This gives some moisture and keeps it from drying out and losing color. It also gives the shell an added luster without being greasy. You can do this to all shells, especially cowries and olives and other smooth species.

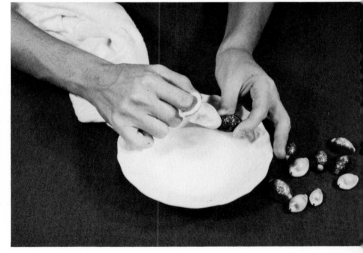

On most of the other species of shells that don't have that shiny finish, we prefer to spray with a light coat of Clear Krylon acrylic spray. We show the use of this in the chapters on jewelry and shell sculptures.

If you choose not to use the spray, the mineral solution and a good buffing with a soft towel or rag will help the shell immensely.

If you have a hobbyist drill, use the
buffer attachment for the same results.

No matter what method you use, your shells are now ready to use in the making of your jewelry and art objects.

Making Shell Jewelry 3

*T*he most exciting time for us, after our first discovery of the shell, is the creation of a piece of jewelry with the shell. This excitement covers even the simplest necklace. The mere act of putting a beautiful or interesting shell on a chain immediately transforms it into something more beautiful and more interesting. It is somewhat like putting a frame (just the right frame) on a picture.

Let us start by making a simple necklace using one shell of your choice. In the following chapter we will proceed to more intricate pieces. The materials and tools you need remain the same. Only your imagination, and the scope of your jewelry stock, can define your limits.

Some of the materials you need you probably have in your home already. The rest are readily obtainable in local hardware or 5 & 10 stores.

Tools and Materials

The basic tools you need are:

One or two 6-inch-long pinch-nose pliers. We use one pair regular pinch-nose pliers from the local 5 & 10, and one professional jewelers' from a good hardware store. The jewelers' pliers has a thinner nose and can get into thin chain to open it easily. The thicker nosed one is good for heavier chain and can close jump rings best.

One small electricians' wire cutters to cut chain that is soldered rather than linked.

An old cuticle scissors and a heavy file to cut or file the jagged edges of some shells.

In Chapter 5 we discuss the use of a hobbyist (high-speed) drill. But this tool is not necessary here.

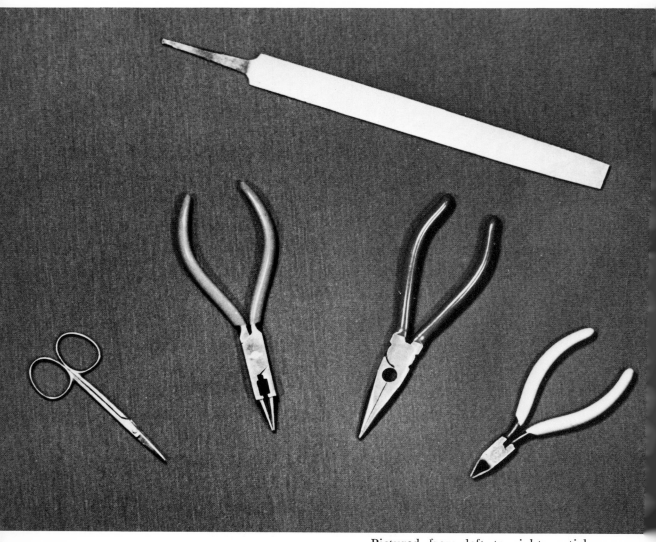

Pictured from left to right: cuticle scissors, jewelers' pinch-nose pliers, regular pinch-nose (or long-nose) pliers, wire cutters. Across the top: Heavy file.

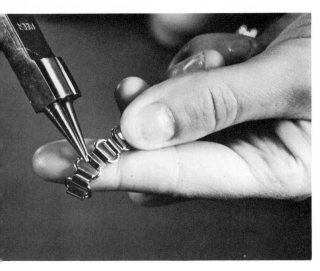

Opening chain with a jewelers' pinch-nose pliers.

ADHESIVES

After experimenting with different adhesives, including very expensive ones specifically recommended by jewelers who work in stones and pearls, we found that a good 5-minute epoxy works best with shells. The one we recommend is made by Devcon.

It is worth the extra effort of mixing the two tubes. Its holding power is just right for the composition of shells. And the 5-minute variety of epoxy does not impede your desire to get on with your project. Just as an artist might choose to work with acrylics rather than oils, the 5-minute epoxy allows you to continue to the next stop without that long wait necessitated by the traditional 24-hour epoxy.

Epoxy, toothpicks, and Q-Tip swabs for applicators, with plastic paper on which to mix epoxy. Plastic shelving paper, an old piece of glass, and a plate are good materials to mix the epoxy on, as they are nonporous.

KRYLON SPRAY

Many shells are perfectly finished in their natural state, such as cowries and olives.

But some shells look better with a thin coat of clear acrylic spray. Another use for the spray is to retard tarnish on inexpensive jewelry chains and findings that have not been gold plated. This certainly is easier than the old "clear nailpolish trick." We found Krylon Crystal Clear acrylic spray to be the best. It dries quickly and has no sticky feeling afterward.

Styrofoam pieces and empty egg cartons.

The easiest way to hold the shells while gluing or working on them and keep your hands free for other work is to use pieces of Styrofoam. Just dig out your own holes. We got ours from the wrapping that came with our new stereo set. And the larger shells fit beautifully into empty egg cartons.

You may discover other objects perfect for shell holding around your home.

JEWELRY FINDINGS

Jewelry findings cover the whole area of chains, jump rings, bell caps, rings, earring wires or backings, and just about anything you need to mount the shell into a piece of jewelry.

The Yellow Pages of the telephone book has listings of finding houses (under Jewelry). In the Index of Supplies in this book we list some finding houses who will send you a catalogue, and who will service small orders such as you would need to begin.

In Chapter 5 we discuss alternatives to jewelry findings, but in this chapter we use the following assortment:

Bell caps—the most useful sizes. These bell caps fit over the top of the shell to give you an attractive means of attaching the shell to a piece of jewelry. The bell cap is glued on using the epoxy we discussed earlier.

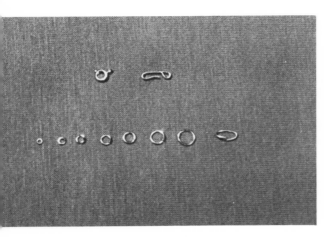

Jump rings—a large assortment of sizes.
These are used to attach the bell cap to the chain.
The top row contains a snap ring to the left, and a hook on the right. These are used with the jump rings to fasten the necklace around the neck.

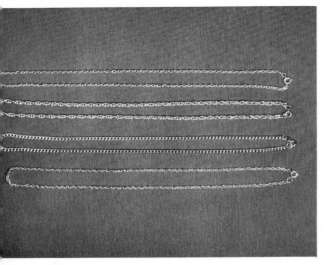

Ready-made chains that may be purchased.

Chains by the foot—they must be cut or opened. The advantages of buying chain this way are many. One advantage is that there are a great many more styles available. Another is that you can easily vary the length and styling of your pieces. Another point to consider is that if you are going to make several chains you save a great deal of money by buying in this manner.

To Make a Simple Shell Necklace

Select the shell or shells you want to use for the necklace and set them up in the Styrofoam bases or egg cartons.

Pick the best-size bell cap for each shell. You should choose one that is large enough to get a good grip on the shell and yet one that looks attractive as an integral part of the jewelry, and is not too overwhelming for the shell.

You can "bell" approximately ten to twelve shells at one time, before the epoxy gets too sticky to use. As you continue "belling" you pick up momentum and can increase the number of shells you bell. Your only limitation is the characteristics of epoxy, which stays at a good spreading consistency for only about three minutes at normal room temperatures.

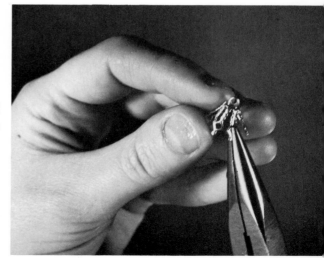

With pliers, spread and shape the bell cap you selected to fit the top of the shell.

When all the shells have a bell cap sitting on them or next to them, spread a strip about ¾ to 1 inch long from each of the two epoxy tubes. This will be more than enough for ten shells.

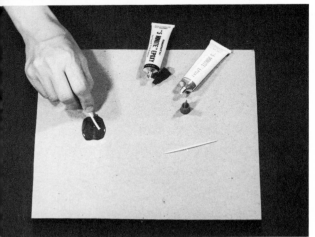

When you are ready to "bell," mix the two strips of epoxy very well with a toothpick or broken Q-Tip swab.

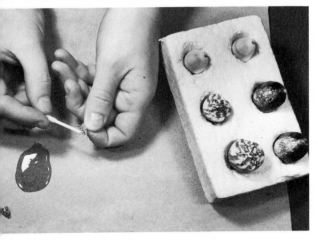

Swab the inside surface of each bell cap.

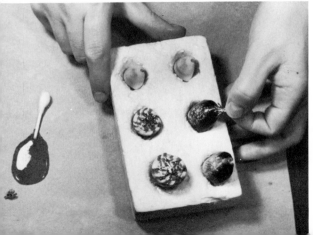

Then place the bell cap on the shell.

Stop when the epoxy begins to get hard to pick up on your applicator. Within five minutes the remaining circle of epoxy on the plastic paper will be as hard as plastic. Now the shell can be removed from the Styrofoam base.

If any prongs from the bell are not tight against the shell, you can pinch them in with the pliers. Or if a portion of the bell cap seems to be "epoxyless," you might have to mix up a dab more and touch up with a toothpick or thin wire (hairpin).

At this point some shells will be ready to put on the neck chain. Other shells, which do not have a bright or smooth surface, you might wish to give a thin coat of clear acrylic spray.

This spray enhances the shell as jewelry, by bringing out the natural color, or by giving a dull shell some sparkle. By all means, if the shell appeals to you in its natural finish, don't do anything to change that finish.

After a few minutes of drying time, the shell is ready for a jump ring through the hole in the bell cap and then for the neck chain of your choice.

Keep the size of the jump ring in proportion to the neck chain you use. A thin chain could use an approximately 3 millimeter (inner diameter), a heavier chain about a 4 or 5 millimeter jump ring.

If you use ready-made chain you usually have a choice of 18-, 20-, and 24-inch lengths.

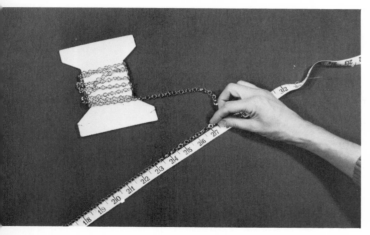

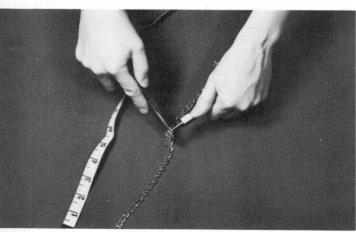

If you buy chain by the foot you might prefer a different length. We found for a thin chain and a small shell a 27-inch length is excellent, with a heavier chain and a larger shell, a 30-inch length.

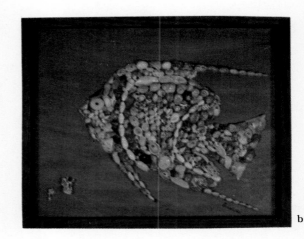

a Model Susan Staff wearing the Leni II piece and matching earrings made with tiger's eyes, which are cut from the chambered nautilus.

b An angelfish made from shells.

c A bird picture that was described in Chapter 6.

d A scorpion conch shell on driftwood with a shale base.

a

b

c

d

a An assortment of heavy 30-inch chain necklaces.

b A shadow box with a flower scene made from shells on a textured wallpaper backing.

c A millipede conch on a very interesting piece of driftwood.

d An assortment of suede pendants.

If you cut your own chain you also need a jump ring at both ends of the chain, and either a hook or snap ring at one of the ends to fasten it. These are easily put on with the pinch-nose pliers.

When we make our 30-inch chain necklaces, we skip the hooks or snap rings and just attach the ends of the chain to each other, as this is a comfortable length to slip over the head.

The final touch to your necklace is attaching the shell with a jump ring to the center of the finished chain.

Complete 30-inch necklace with Diana conch shell from the Indo-Pacific.

Finished 30-inch heavy chain necklaces.

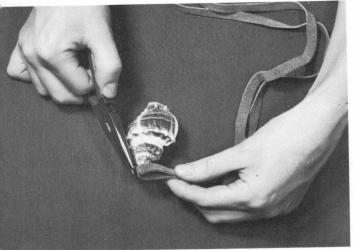

Instead of metal chain you can attach the shell via jump ring to strips of leather, suede, twine, ribbon, macramé, to mention several variations on a theme. Make the strips approximately 33 to 36 inches in length. A good width is ¼ inch. Tie them in a square knot so they can be easily slipped over the head.

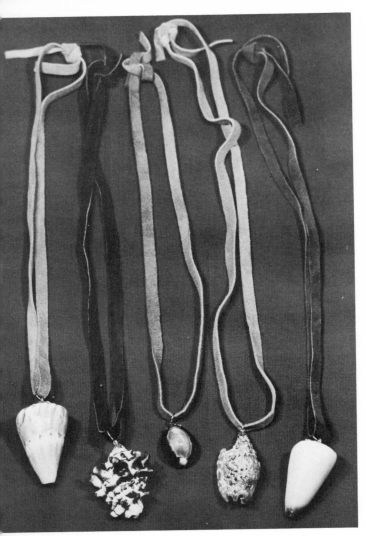

Finished suede necklaces.

More Complex Pieces **4**

*n*ow that you see the possibilities available to you with the jewelry findings and shells, let's get a little more variety and gradually work up to some more complex pieces.

Chokers

For the time being, let's keep the pieces simple by starting with some chokers, using suede, leather, or ribbon.

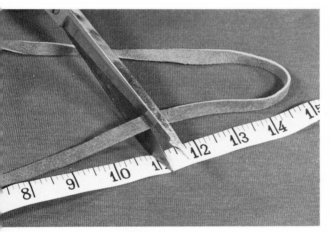

Cut the material you wish to use as a choker (in this case a strip of suede). An average choker length is 11 inches with a 4½-inch end chain. But since your jewelry is custom made, you can measure your neck and cut a suitable length for yourself.

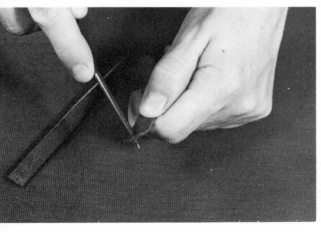

Punch holes at both ends of the strip with the point of a scissors or a leather hole puncher.

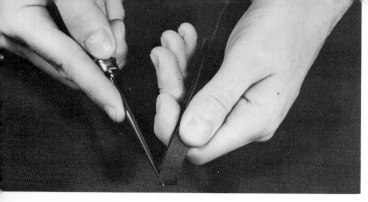

Punch a hole just off center of the strip. This is where the shell will hang.

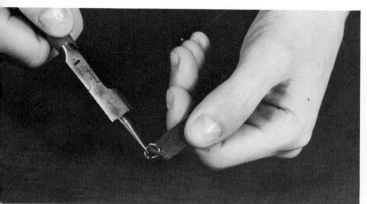

Fit jump rings through the end holes and close them.

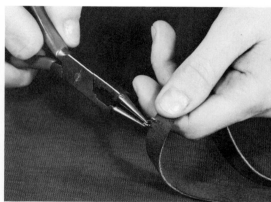

Fit a jump ring through the center hole.

Add the shell before closing the jump ring.

At one end, add a hook to the jump ring.

At the other end add 4½ inches of end chain to make the choker adjustable. You can eliminate this chain if you wish by measuring your strip exactly to your neck width, and then just close by hooking to jump ring.

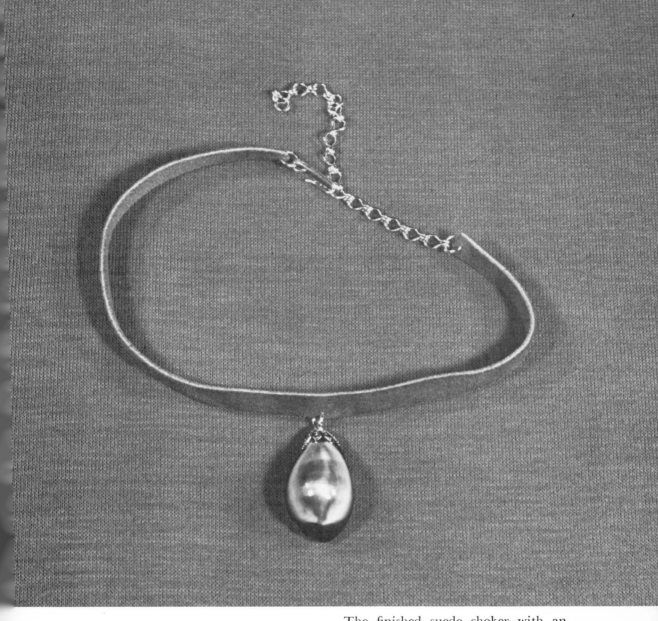

The finished suede choker with an onyx cowrie.

You can make a choker with chain as well. This, of course, has a dressier **look**.

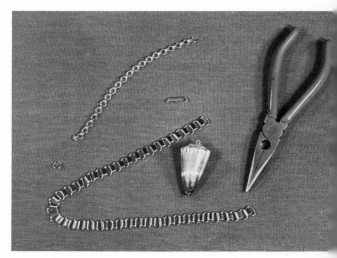

The materials needed are a chain, an end chain, jump rings, a hook, and pinch-nose pliers.

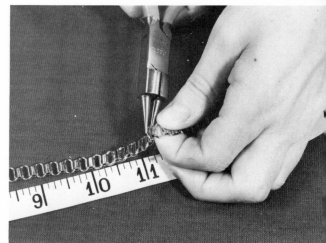

Open the chain to desired choker length.

Attach the hook to one end and the end chain to the other.

Then add the shell to the near center by means of a jump ring.

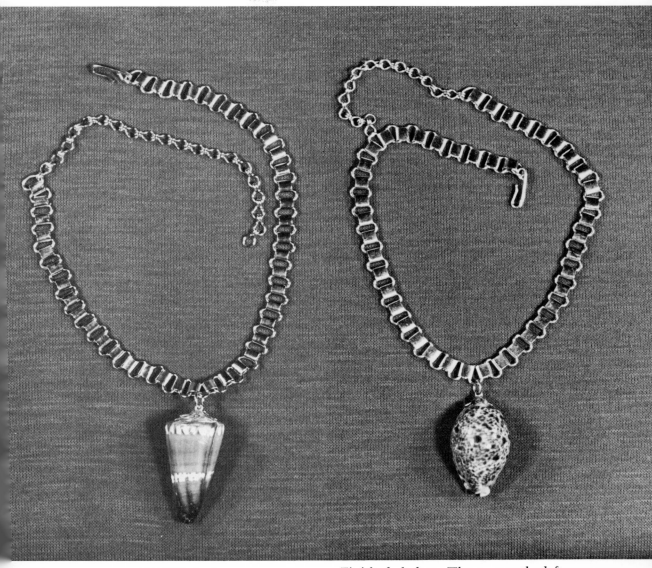

Finished chokers. The one on the left has a cone shell, and the one on the right has a lynx cowrie.

You can get as complex as you wish by adding more shells around. Here is a choker with three shells.

Here are some with six shells.

CLEO

A step beyond the previous chokers is one with several shells dangling at various lengths from additional chains.

One of our versions of this we call the Cleo, as it reminded us of something Cleopatra might have worn.

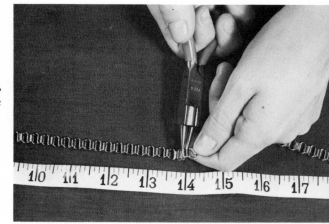

This choker should hang a little lower, and so we suggest that you cut the chain at 14 inches or more.

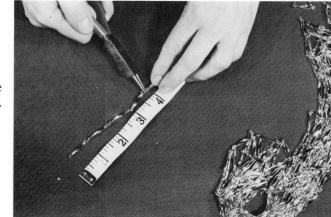

Using a complementing chain, cut one piece approximately 4 inches long. This will be the center piece.

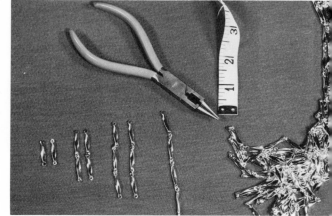

Then cut two chains slightly shorter (3 inches). Then two more chains at 2 inches. And then two more chains at 1 inch.

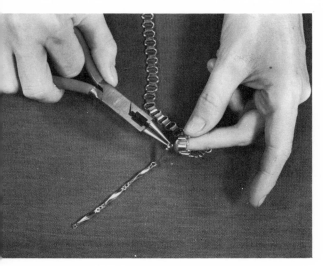

Attach the longest (4-inch) chain to the center of the choker chain. (That is 7 inches from one side, if the chain you cut was 14 inches.)

Then attach the next two chains (the 3-inch ones), one on either side of the center chain, approximately 1 inch away. On our choker chain we count 4 disks distance on either side.

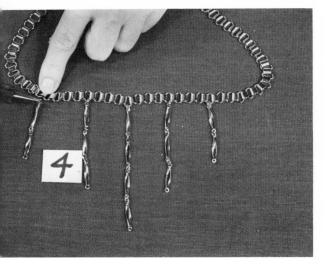

The next two chains (2-inch lengths) we attach 4 disks away from the previous ones, one on either side again.

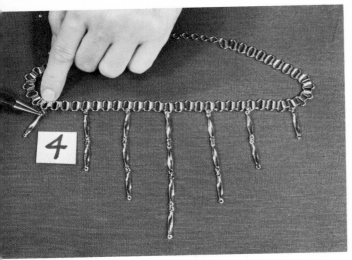

The last two chains (1-inch lengths) are attached another 4 disks away on either side.

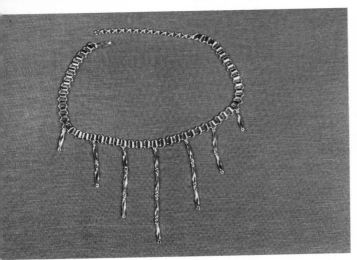

The finished Cleo, with a hook added at one end and 4½ inches of end chain at the other.

Then have fun adding your shells. We use a magnificent center shell, and then try to find matching pairs for the rest of the lengths. If you can't find shells that match, try to at least have them get smaller and smaller as the chain gets shorter and shorter. This carries out the look of the piece.

The Cleo looks especially good on a low scoop neckline. But it can be worn equally well on a high turtleneck.

BIB

Another variation on the choker idea is what we call a bib.

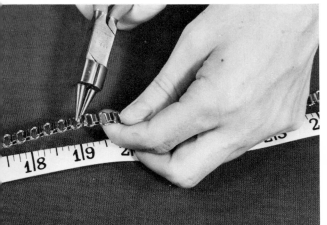

We cut this choker even longer at 19 inches, and thus eliminate the end chain. It can still be adjusted to any length because of the nature of the chain we use.

The materials needed are a choker chain 19 inches long, and a thinner chain, such as an end chain, that works very well for this piece. You need three pieces 7 inches each, for the drapes; jump rings, and an end hook.

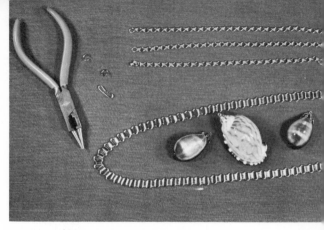

Attach one of the thin chain pieces 5 inches in from the end of the choker chain, after first attaching the hook.

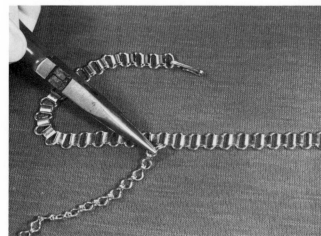

Then with jump ring attached to the other end of this first drape, and one end of the second drape . . .

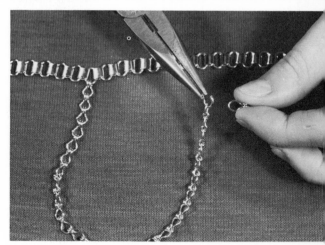

attach the jump ring approximately 3 inches (or 10 disks) in from the first jump ring.

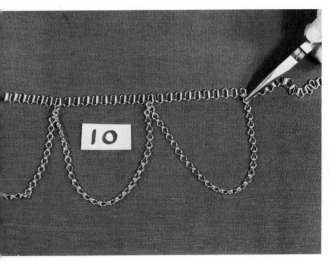

Repeat the above step with the third drape, and then attach the end of the third drape at another 3-inch (or 10-disk) separation.

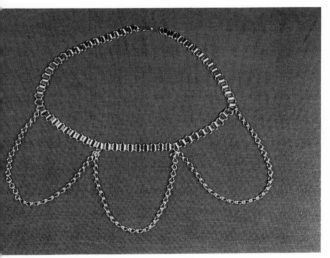

This gives you three drapes of equal distance in the center of the bib piece.

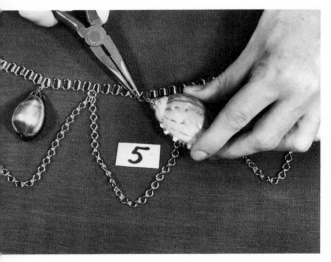

Add the shells to the center of each drape. (Here 5 disks in.)

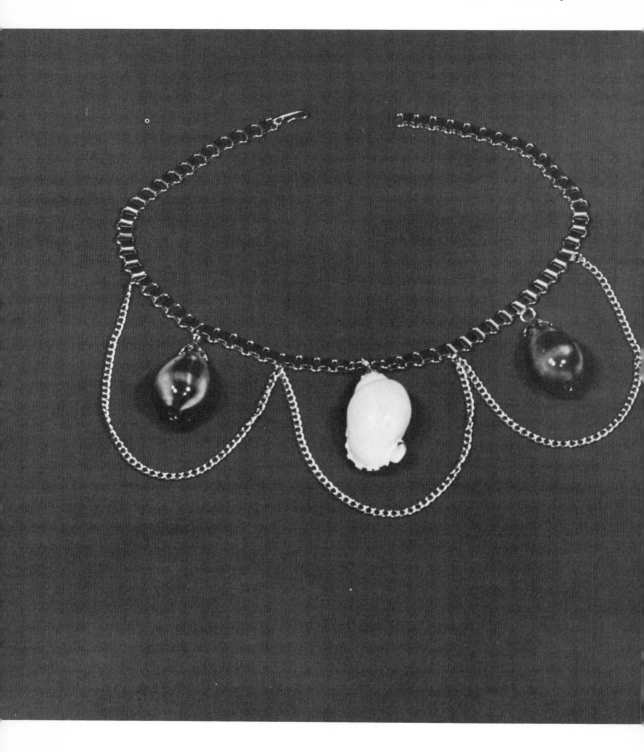

Finished bib pieces.

Belt

A beautiful belt can be made using the same idea as the bib.

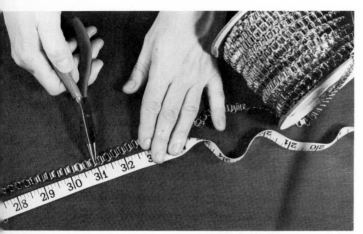

Cut your chain to fit your belt size. (Average is about 31 inches.)

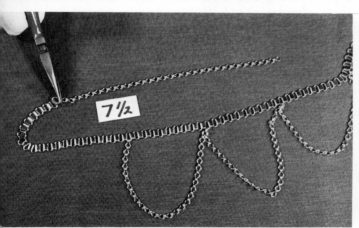

Add approximately 7½ inches of end chain to one end, and at about 7 inches in from that end chain, make the three drapes as described for the bib.

Add a hook to the end chain.

Add a hook to the other end of the belt as well.

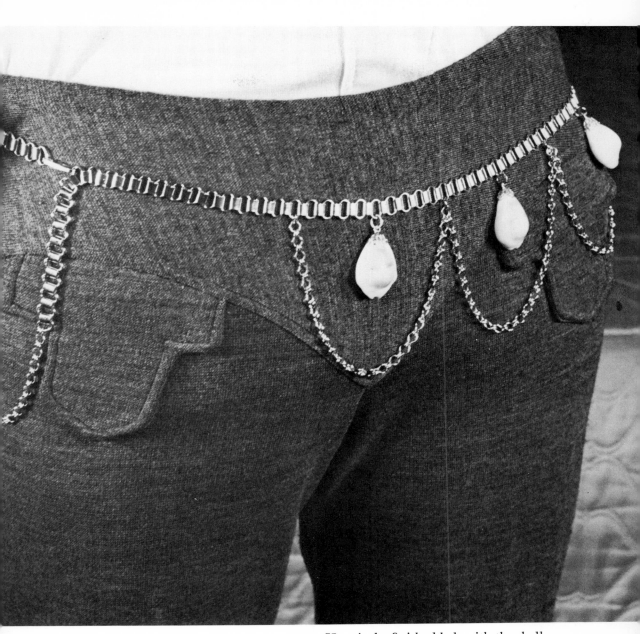

Here is the finished belt with the shells added. Note how the hook at the end of the end chain allows you to adjust the belt size and then hooks up to make another drape.

Another idea for a belt is to cut a length of chain to fit your waist. Add a hook to one end and a shell to the other, and hang shells at set intervals along the length of the chain. This belt has seven money cowries on it.

Bracelets

Bracelets are very easy to make.

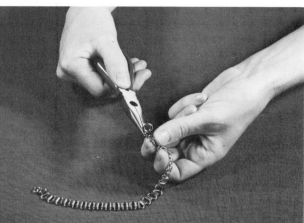

Cut a piece of chain to fit your wrist. At one end attach a jump ring, and at the other end a clasp.

Then attach a small shell, or two, or several shells at intervals around the bracelet.

Finished bracelets.

Cuff Links

It is very easy to make exquisite cuff links from shells, shell scrapings, or cuttings. The only prerequisite is that the shell have a relatively flat underside, so that it will sit on a backing.

We use a cuff link with a ½-inch or 13-millimeter round disk soldered on. Finding companies usually have smaller disks also, but the smaller disk doesn't have enough surface for the epoxy to get a good grip on the shell.

We have not as yet located a ready-made cuff link backing or ring with prongs or cage effect, in which the shells would fit, as each shell is different in size and shape (even in the same species). Perhaps you will be luckier in your search than we have been.

The cuff links we make and recommend to you are very handsome, durable, and quite simple to make.

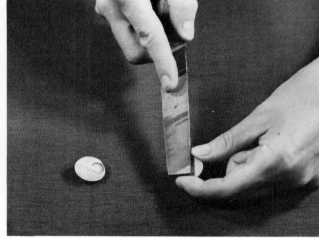

Pick shells like cowries, or shell cuttings or parts like cat's eyes.

With hobbyist drill or hand file, roughen the back of shell so that the epoxy can adhere better to it.

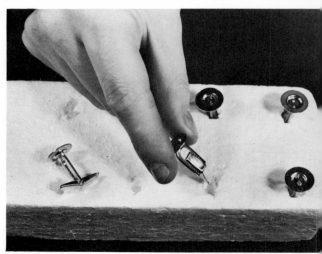

Mount cuff link backings into Styrofoam or other such base to hold them firmly, and leave your hands free to work.

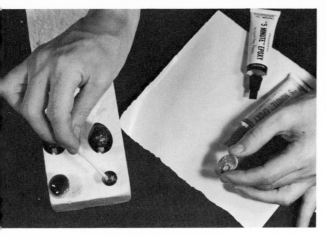

Mix your epoxy and lightly cover each disk.

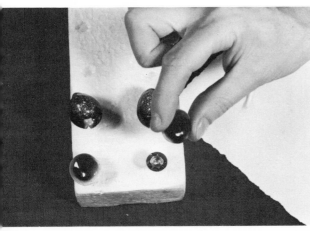

Place shells firmly on disks. In a few minutes the epoxy will dry and you have a pair of shell cuff links.

Finished cuff links. *Bottom row:* A variety of cowries.
Middle row: Cat's eye.
Top row: Mother-of-pearl scrapings from a shell.

Earrings

Earrings are also rather easy to make.

Match up by size and coloring as closely as possible two shells that you think would make pretty earrings.

We usually use small cowries (such as the snake, money, or ringtop), or if you can get the tiger's eyes (sometimes called nautilus drops, as they are cut from the chambered nautilus from the Philippine Islands area). They are getting hard to find and thus rather expensive when you do come across them. But they make the most beautiful earrings and pendants imaginable.

We have used many other shells, including small cones and even small murex shells. Many times we make matched earrings to go with our necklaces.

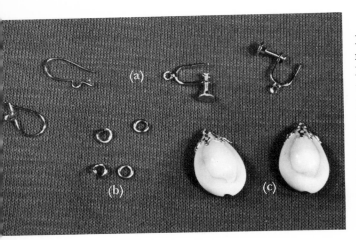

Here are the findings necessary to make a simple pair of earrings: (a) Pierced or non-pierced backings. Note that the non-pierced backings have a pierced look, with a circle at the base on which to hang the shell. The pierced earrings we use are a .018 thickness, 14-karat gold earwire with a loop for the shell. (b) Small size jump rings (.½ or .1). (c) Shells with bell caps epoxied on.

If you prefer, you could choose an earring backing on which you can epoxy the shell, rather than have it hanging down. But remember, this limits you to shells with relatively flat undersides.

Attach the first jump ring to the opening in the bell cap and close it.

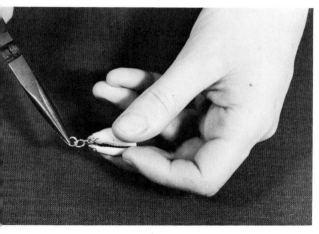

Attach a second jump ring to the first and close it also. You need the two jump rings so that the shell hangs frontward, rather than twisted sideward.

Hang the top jump ring in the loop of the earwire, or through the ring in the screw-on type. *Voilà,* you have a finished pair of earrings.

If you wish to have the shells hang lower, we suggest you use a delicate chain. The particular one we use here is soldered and thus requires a small wire cutter to open the links. The other chain can be opened with the pinch-nose pliers.

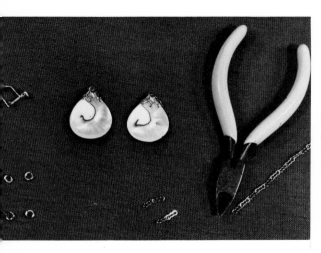

Here we are using the tiger's eyes we spoke of earlier. Cut the chain according to how long you want the earring to hang.

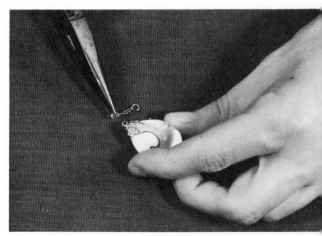

As this chain is soldered we have to add a small jump ring at each end, one to enable us to attach it to the bell cap on the tiger's eye . . .

and one on the other end so that the shell will hang forward. Here we are using the screw-on type backing.

If you want to make a little more intricate variety, search through the "findings" catalogues for different chains from which to dangle shells.

Now we show some gold-plated bars, $1\frac{3}{4}$ or $1\frac{5}{8}$ inches long, used in some interesting designs for earrings.

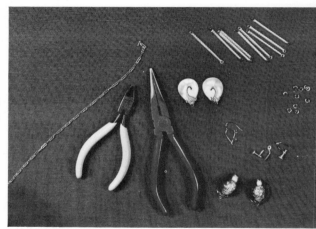

Here are the bars, some chains, the shells in pairs, the backings, jump rings, and pliers and cutters.

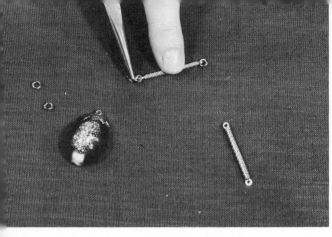

This pair of earrings is going to hang from a 1¾-inch bar with a small jump ring at each end.

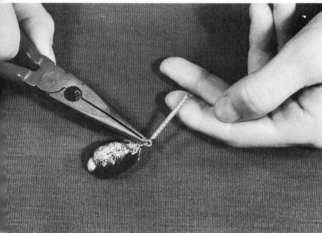

Attach one end to the shell . . .

and the other end to the loop in the earring backing.

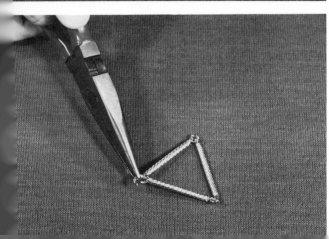

Here we are making a triangle from three of these bars (an idea we use later in a necklace).

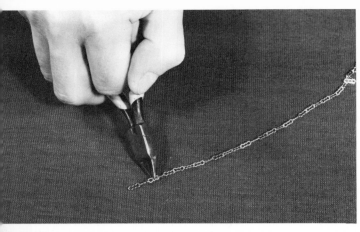

Again we are using the soldered chain . . .

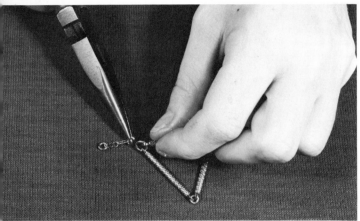

with a jump ring at each end; one to hang the triangle from and the other to attach to the earring backing.

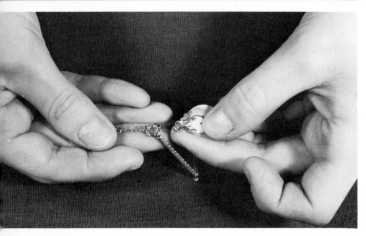

Then we attach a shell by means of a jump ring to the inside of the triangle. You need a very narrow shell to fit inside the triangle.

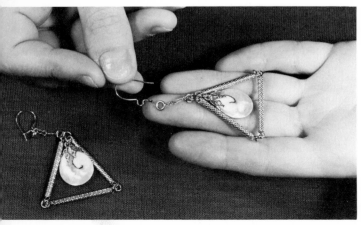

And finally, attach the other end to the earring backing.

An assortment of earrings using the methods described above.

Our model, Susan Staff, wearing a
pair of triangle earrings.

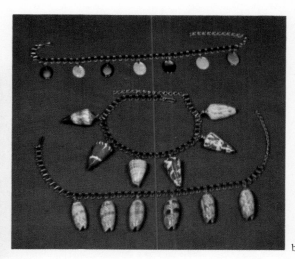

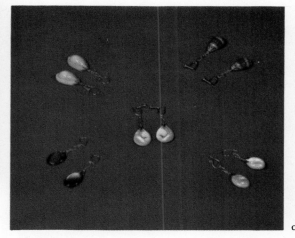

Model wearing the Cleopatra neckpiece and the three-shell belt.

An assortment of six shell chokers with pearlized cuttings from shells *(top)*, with cone shells *(middle)*, with olive shells *(bottom)*.

c An assortment of earrings made with pearlized cuttings from shells, tiger's eyes, and cowrie shells.

d An assortment of cuff links made with pearlized cuttings from shells, cat's eyes, and cowrie shells.

a

b

d

FROM THE COLLECTION OF GLORIA VANDERBILT

a Two swans made from shells.

b A cross made from shells. On the left are a mini
ature piano and chair and a book cover covere
in mother-of-pearl cut from shells, and in fro
a shell belt.

c Two large floral arrangements made entire
from shells. An 18th-century Spanish antiqu

d A jewel box made in Mexico by one of the loc
craftsmen.

Various Pendants and
More Intricate Neckpieces

Now we are back to making a necklace from the bars, using the same delicate chain we used in the earrings.

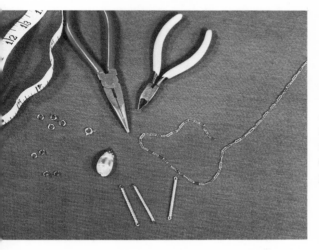

Materials include the chain, bars (this time we are using the larger ones, 1⅝ inches, which give us a little more leeway in the size of the shells inserted). Also, a snap ring to close the necklace, jump rings, medium size (.2 or .3), and your tools: tape measure, pliers, and small wire cutters.

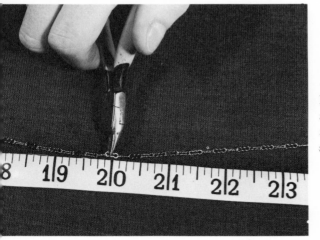

For a simple triangle pendant, we cut a 20- or 24-inch length of chain and attach a jump ring to one end and a snap ring (or hook) to the other.

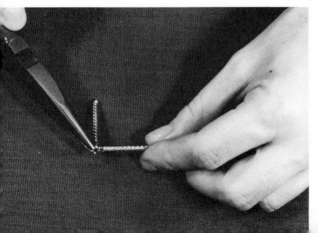

Then we make the triangle by attaching, first, two bars with a jump ring.

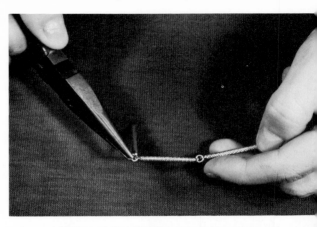

Then a third bar with a jump ring.

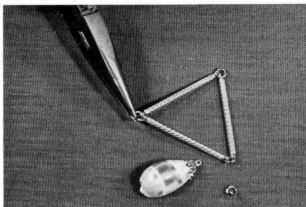

And finally, attaching the first and third bars together in the form of a triangle, with a larger jump ring.

After hanging a shell in the center of the triangle by means of another jump ring, we attach the chain to the triangle with a third jump ring.

A variation on the above is what we call the double triangle.

Start to make the triangle, but add another bar along with the third one.

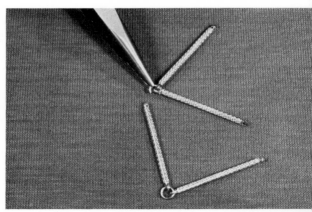

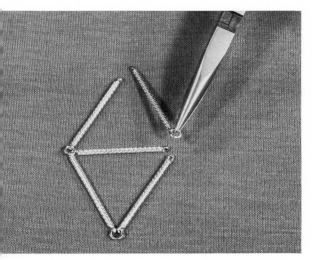

And then another bar at the other end.

And then attach the two bars of the inverted triangle with a jump ring. Then attach a shell inside the top triangle, and one below the inverted triangle.

And then add your necklace chain as you did in the single triangle.

Left: Finished single and double triangles.

Susan Staff wearing a double triangle and earrings that match one of the shells in the necklace.

If you fall in love with these bars as we did, you might want to try the following designs also.

This one we call the Iron Cross. It is a six-sided pendant and will be one of the highlights of your jewelry case.

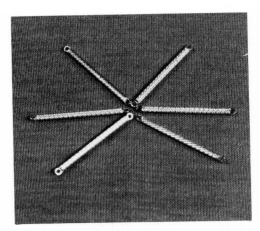

Start with six bars.

Attach them with a medium-size jump ring (about a .3), as a shell is also going to need room to hang from it.

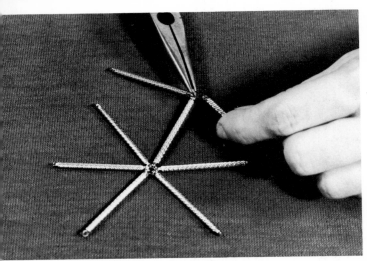

Then spread the six bars out like the rays of the sun, and begin to attach bars to the outer ends to form an enclosed pattern. First add two bars as above.

Then add one more bar to the second one.

Then another bar to the third one.

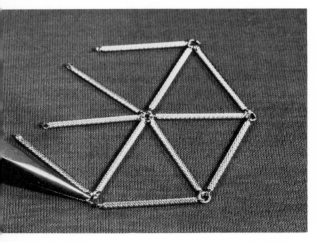

Then another bar to the fourth one.

And another bar to the fifth one.

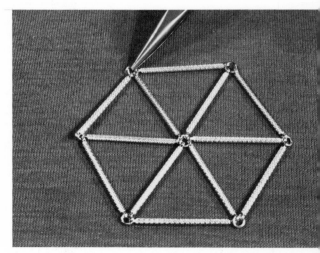

And last, the sixth bar attaches to the other end of the first bar.

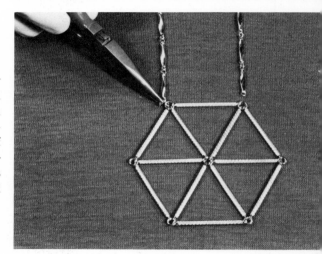

Then add a necklace chain of your choice to the two top triangles formed by the pattern. Note that the chain you use will have to be cut in two sections as it is attached to two sides of the piece. If you want a 20-inch necklace, which is a good length for this design, you must cut two lengths of 10 inches.

Finally add a shell to the center of the two top triangles, and one to the center jump ring which forms the top of the bottom triangle.

Finished Iron Cross with tiger's eyes.

Here are some ideas for more intricate designs so that you can see the un-limited range of design available.

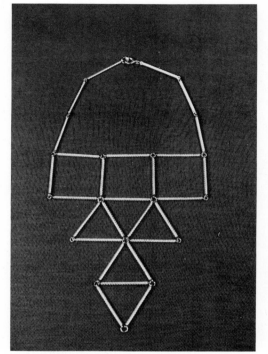

This we call the Leni I.

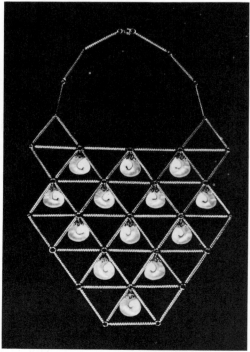

This is an extension of the preceding piece which we call the Leni II.

Leni I with shells added, on model, with matching earrings.

Here is an abalone shell attached by bell caps to a 24-inch chain. Four shells are dangling from various-length chains, attached to the abalone through its natural holes (by jump rings or by epoxying bell caps from the underside of the abalone). Another idea is to just use the abalone hanging from a chain, without the additional shells.

There is no end to the variety of designs you can come up with. You will probably find an interesting chain or other type of finding by looking through the catalogues you can send for from the finding companies listed in the Index of Supplies. And from the findings you select, you will make your own designs and patterns for your jewelry and have a marvelous time doing so.

Our only advice is have fun, and don't be afraid to experiment.

Alternate Methods of Making Jewelry 5

*F*rom the previous chapters you have seen how easily shells become exquisite pieces of jewelry when applied to the right findings. In this chapter, we want to show you other ways to make your shells into fascinating pieces of jewelry, without the use of standard jewelry findings, in case these findings prove difficult to obtain in your area, and also, as you will see, because a different effect is created in the styling of these pieces.

In ancient times natives of various countries and, more recently, Indians of this country wore necklaces of shells strung together. If you visit a tropical island today, you will also find many examples of these kinds of work being sold by the natives. In fact some of our friends, who were stationed in the Pacific during World War II, made similar necklaces with the shells they picked up on the beaches.

The methods of working with shells described in this chapter are well suited to the common shells you might pick up along the beaches of North America (as well as in freshwater lakes and rivers), as they carry out a more rustic theme, rather than a jewel-like effect achieved in the previous chapters.

A variety of shells that can easily be used in making jewelry by these methods. *Bottom row:* Pectens, keyhole limpets, strombus. *Second row:* Clam, abalone, donkey's ear abalone. *Top row:* Bubble shell, tellin clam.

Drilling, Boring, and Stringing

Prepare and clean your shells as described in Chapter 2. Let's begin with the simplest pendant and then graduate to more complicated combinations.

If it is possible to obtain a hobbyist drill, do so. This is a lightweight, high-speed drill that will be invaluable to you in working with shells. Because it works at such high speed it will not crack the shell.

The drill pictured is a Dremel High Speed (30,000 rpm) Standard Hobbyist Drill.

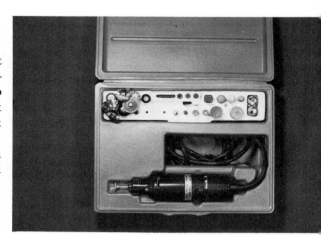

Plastic eyeglasses, drill, and various bits and polishers to use with the drill.

When using the drill always use eyeglasses to protect your eyes from shell fragments and dust.

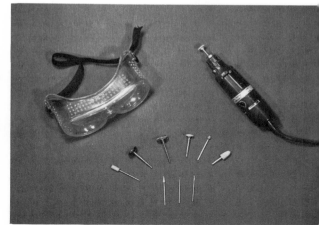

There are many bits and burrs that come with a hobbyist drill. Some are used for drilling large holes, some are for sanding and polishing, some are for cutting. By experimenting, you will soon become acquainted with the ones that suit your various needs.

Start with a small-tipped burr, and if you find that the hole is too small you can try the next size burr.

Additional bits and burrs may be purchased at a minimal cost at any good hobby shop or dental supply house. Or if you have a nice dentist, as we do, he might give you some of his old burrs. Also you can order them directly from the drill manufacturer (*see* Index of Supplies).

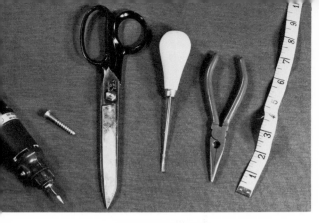

Materials needed. A drill, or large screw, scissors, awl, pinch-nose pliers, and tape measure.

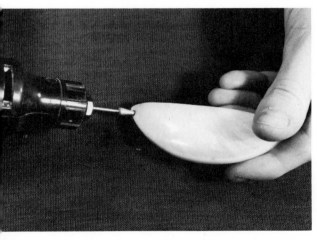

Sometimes you might be able to bore a hole through the shell with a large screw. This is very tedious work and many times damages the shell. So if you can obtain a high-speed drill, so much the better.

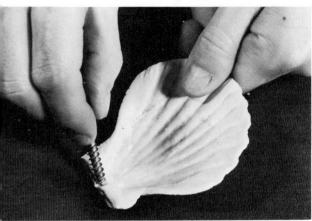

Drilling through a clam-like shell.

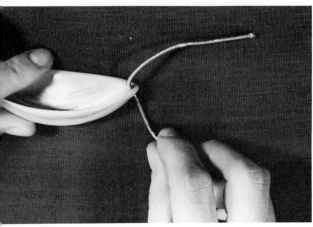

After the hole is drilled, pass a length of cord or string through the hole and tie at the neck as a pendant.

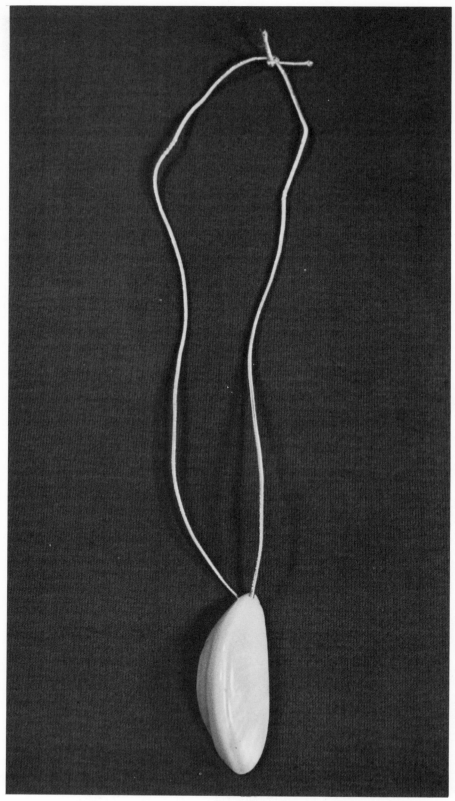

Or make a shorter length to wear as a choker.

After you have made this simple piece, there are infinite variations.

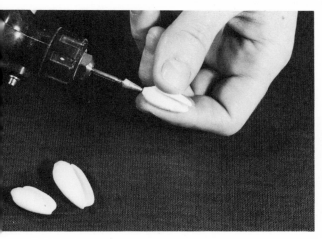

Drilling holes in top end of bubble shells.

String the drilled bubble shells together on an approximate 28- to 34-inch length of string or waxed string (available in stores for stringing beads or pearls).

You can make a knot between each shell if you wish. Or you could even add a wooden bead or other type of bead or stone or many other shells between each bubble shell to make an interesting contrast.

Finished bubble necklace.

Here are two more strung shell neck-laces. These were made in the Philip-pine Islands.

Here is a variation without the use of drilling a hole in the shell. This method would work very well on the bubble shell and on the cowrie shell, which we have used here.

Using picture hanging wire, cut a length for each shell in the necklace a little longer than the shell at each end.

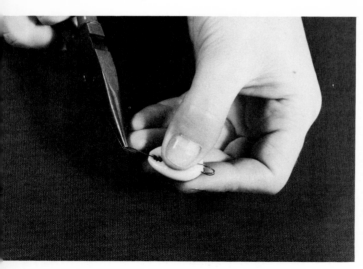

Wrap the wire around itself to form a circle at each end of the shell.

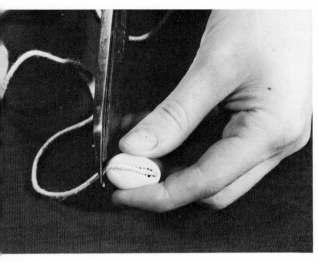

Cut a length of heavy string to fit snugly inside each shell.

Stuff the string (with Elmer's glue on it) inside the opening of the shell, to hold the wire inside.

When one shell is finished make the next shell and wrap the wire around the circle of the previous shell and keep doing this until the necklace is completed. At the end you can add an additional shell hanging downward wrapped around the two end circles.

Completed necklace except for clasp.
You can add string to tie, or a jump
ring and hook from a discarded necklace, or from a hobby shop or a kit,
or make a hook from the wire.

A necklace made in the Philippines by drilling the ends of each shell (in this case a tiger's eye cutting) and attaching each shell to the next with a U-shaped wire and closing the U with pliers each time. Notice they have used a jewelers' clasp at the back to fasten.

Wire Wrapping

Another simple and even more interesting method to convert a shell into a necklace is wire wrapping. This method can be used if you don't have a drill, or if you don't want to mar the shell with a hole. It is effective on bivalves as well as univalves.

You'll need various necklace materials: suede strips, ready-made chain, a roll of picture hanging wire, two types of cord, and a leather strip. You can also get gold wire in rolls for use here.

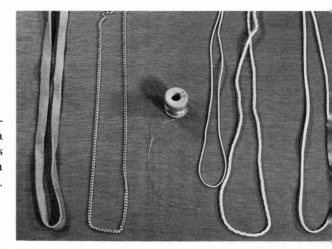

Simply start wrapping the wire around your shell (in this case a strombus).

Make sure to make a cage that will support the shell and hold it firmly.

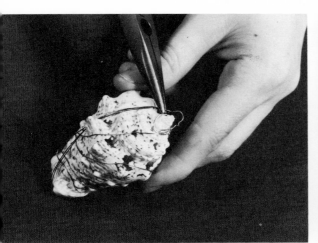

Make a loop at the top and tie off wire. You can reinforce the piece by dabbing Elmer's glue in some areas where the wire touches the shell.

Pass the necklace material of your choice through the loop and tie at the top.

Completed shell on a leather strip.

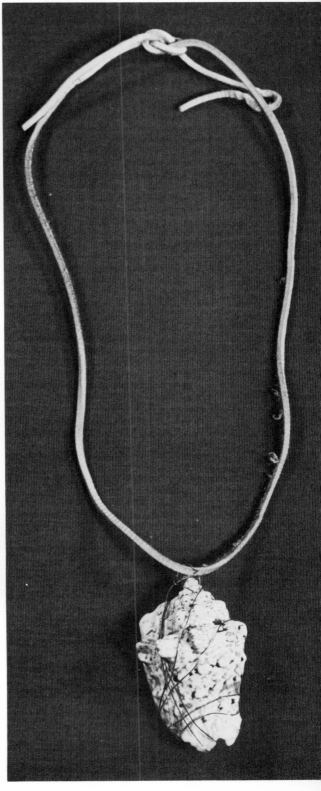

You probably will come up with some interesting variations of your own using the materials you have at hand and, of course, depending on the shells you have to work with.

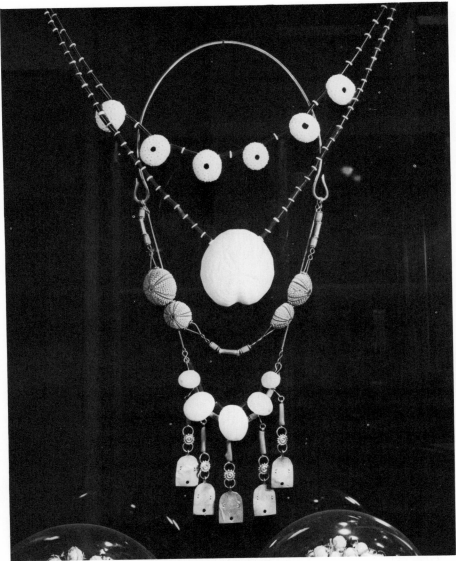

Here are two necklaces from the Gloria Vanderbilt collection. The top one is a double strand of leather with sea urchin skeletons tied onto it at intervals, with a sand dollar in the center of the bottom strand. The second necklace uses wire threaded through sea urchins, beads, and pieces of metal.

Projects

HEADBAND

The Indians wore headbands made with shells and the style seems to be in vogue again.

Here is a simple way to make a headband, or dress up an already existing headband, with a shell as the focal point.

First measure the size of your head across the forehead. Then cut to size either chain or suede or any other type of material you wish.

Here we are using a crocheted band and just adding a short length (1½ inches) of chain (or rope) by means of jump rings.

Then attach the shell.

Here is Leni Goodman wearing the completed headband.

If you use chain or suede instead, just follow the directions for a choker in the last chapter.

A small shell such as a cowrie seems to lie best as it is flat on one side.

BELTS AND BUCKLES

Using any found or bought material you can make lovely belts using a shell as a centerpiece or buckle.

Here is a strip of snakeskin that we bought, cut to size for a belt, and added a lining of material and eye hooks to close. Then we drilled two slots through a scorpion conch to use as a buckle (as you can see by the additional shell in the picture). We threaded the scorpion between the snakeskin and the lining and sewed them together.

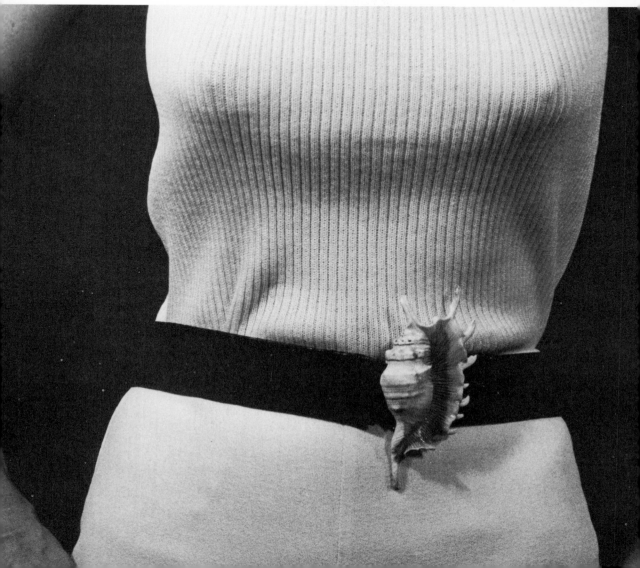

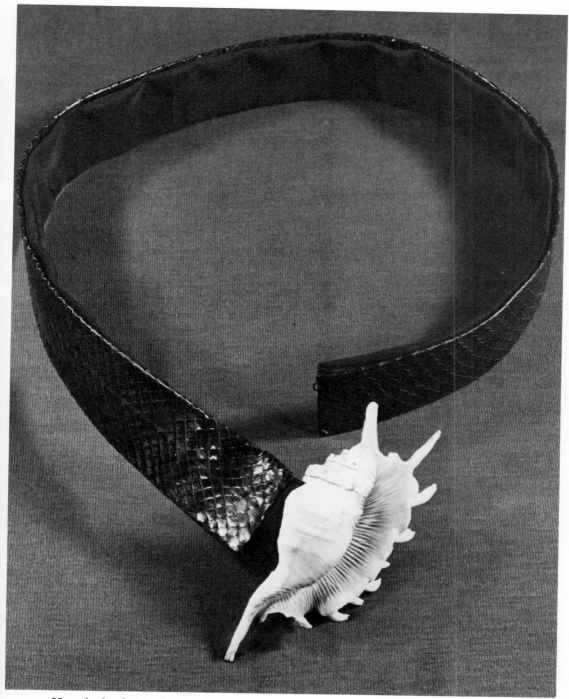

Here is the finished belt with the shell
in place.

Left: You can see what a unique belt
this makes.

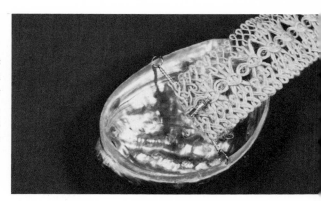

Here is another belt idea. Drill a hole on the top and bottom edge of an abalone shell, and attach a metal bar (with jump rings or other means). Then attach your belt material around this bar. Add a hook with which to close the belt.

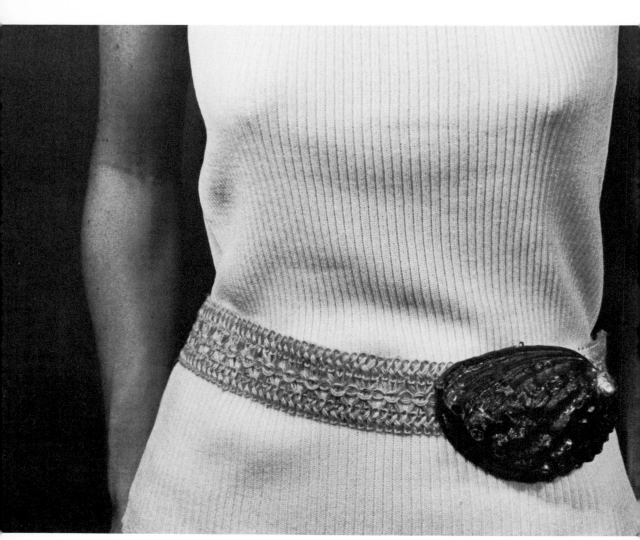

Here is the finished belt with the abalone in place.

Another simple belt idea is to drill holes in some shells and sew them onto any material that you might wish to use as a belt.

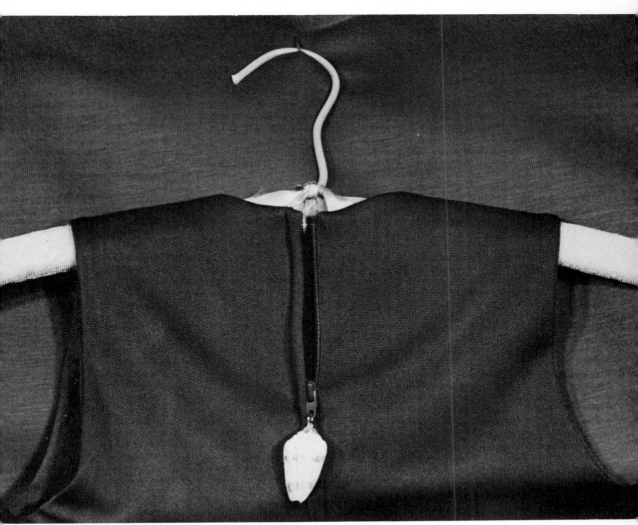

Here is a shell added to the pull ring of a zipper to dress up an outfit.

You can also add a shell to your key-ring.

Shells can also be added to barrettes and other hair ornaments. As you can see, shells can really be added to almost any object. So take advantage of the natural beauty of these wonders of nature.

Shell Pictures, Collages, Shadow Boxes, and Other Art Objects **6**

*S*hell collages and pictures are a great conversation piece when displayed on your wall. The thing we enjoy most about these pictures, apart from the fun in making them, is that here is an interesting way to display all the little shells one collects. They are not tucked away somewhere in a box never to see the light of day again. Rather, they are available to be seen and admired and to remind one of the joy there was in discovering them at the oceanside.

Also a shell collage or picture makes a beautiful gift, and the person receiving it can appreciate and share your love of the beauty of the shells in the form of something you have created for them.

Shell Pictures and Collages

MATERIALS

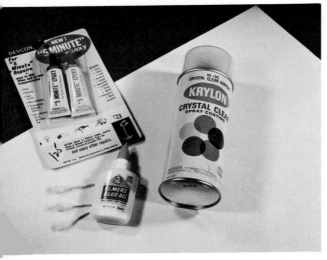

Elmer's Glue-All is the best type of adherent to use because it dries clear, is easy to apply, and does the job of adhering shells to canvas or wood.

Devcon "5 Minute" Epoxy should be used for heavier shells or pieces of driftwood, etc., just to make sure the extra weight will adhere.

Krylon Crystal Clear spray—a thin coating over the finished picture will brighten and preserve the shells.

Canvas board which comes in a variety of sizes is excellent for shell pictures as it takes paint very well and is rigid enough to hold the shells.

Other backings could be ¼-inch plywood or Masonite.

Here are some items you will need to paint the background before adding your shells. Brushes, spreading knife, white primer coat (optional), the tubes of paint you choose to use, pencil or charcoal to outline the picture, linseed oil, turpentine, rag, and paint mixing board.

Other materials needed include a frame. The choice is yours, depending on the amount of money you wish to spend or your handicraft ability. Ready-made frames are abundant in the standard sizes in department, 5 & 10, and art supply stores. They can be bought finished or ready to paint or stain, or even ready to assemble from pieces. Or you might wish to make your own frame.

Instead of the paint materials described above, you might want to cover ¼-inch plywood with some material or paper for the background.

And, of course, the obvious material needed is all the small shells and fragments of shells and coral and sea glass and assorted goodies you might wish to use in your picture.

PAINTING THE BACKGROUND

The first step in making your shell collage or picture is painting in the background.

Mix your paint until you arrive at the shade you wish. This background is a mixture of orange and white which gives us a beautiful goldish color. Use either vertical or horizontal strokes throughout. We are using oil paints, but you could use acrylics or even watercolors. Oils can take approximately two days to dry while the other mediums take only a few hours at the most.

After the canvas board is completely dry, draw the outline of the picture or pattern you wish to make. Perhaps it will be a fish, a flower, a bird—but we do suggest that you start with a simple form. One does not have to be an artist to make a shell collage or picture. Just outline a basic form or a basic area to be filled in with shells. You will be amazed at how the shells take over the picture and compensate for any deficiency in your drawing ability.

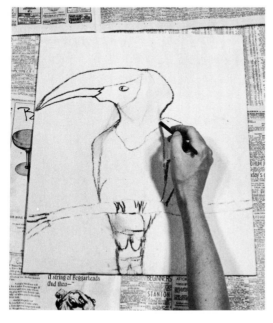

As you can see this is going to be a bird (a hornbill, which we sketched from a color photo in a nature book). Don't worry about being neat as your outline and any of your mistakes are easily covered with shells as you go along, or, if necessary, with paint after the picture is finished.

FILLING IN THE OUTLINE

If you use a color photo or picture to guide you in the outline then by all means use the colors in the picture to help you determine your color scheme with your shells.

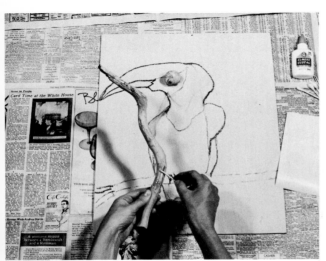

Before we finished laying out all our shells we spied a moon snail that we thought would be perfect for his eye. And also an interesting piece of driftwood to use as the branch on which he was sitting. We use epoxy to adhere the driftwood as it is heavy.

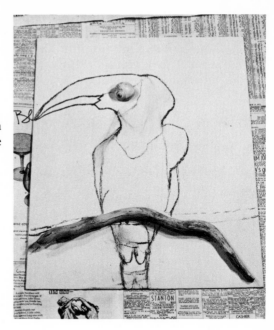

When we finish the picture we can easily paint over the markings for the original branch.

Then we scattered all our shells around on the newspaper so that we could decide on the colors to use in the different areas. Working on an area at a time, we begin to fill in the picture. First spread the Elmer's glue and then lay in the shells. Here we are using all dark shells around the eye area. Remember to overlap the outline as you go along.

We finish the eye area and find a razor clam and a cut fragment of a shell to use for his beak.

Then we begin to fill in the entire top half of his beak with shiny ringtop cowries.

His head is going to be completely covered with purple clam shells in a layered effect to look like feathers.

You can see the layered effect here.
Now we are filling in the body area
with Elmer's glue . . .

and covering this area with assorted
small shells. If there are any spaces
after you have finished you can always
add shells to cover with a dab of glue
on their back.

We are using a featherlike look in the
tail area also, this time with tiny pink
clam shells.

We are adding two ark shells (turkey wings) as his feet, on the driftwood. To make sure they hold, as they are touching only a very small area, we are using the 5-minute epoxy. Add any other shells you might wish to complete the picture.

Now we are touching up all the mistakes we were not able to cover with shells.

Let the picture dry a few hours and then spray with Krylon Crystal Clear spray if you wish. It will give the shells a brighter appearance and help preserve their colors.

Here is the finished picture in its frame.

Here is another shell picture. This angelfish on a sea-green background has a sea urchin for an eye. And his various bands of color and fins are accented with similar shape shells (bubble, flamingo tongue, and augers, mitres, ceriths, etc.). A few bits of coral were added in the corner to complete this underwater scene.

If you enjoy painting you could, of course, paint an entire picture using shells as your inspiration. Here is an abstract painting using the snail shell as a taking-off point. *Artist: Stuart Goodman.*

After you find how easy it is to make a picture or collage using a simple form, you might want to try an abstract. Using the same technique, just fit your shells and coral into your picture scheme and away you go.

Here are some other ways to use shells in a picture, especially if you have specimen quality shells and wish to display them in an exciting manner.

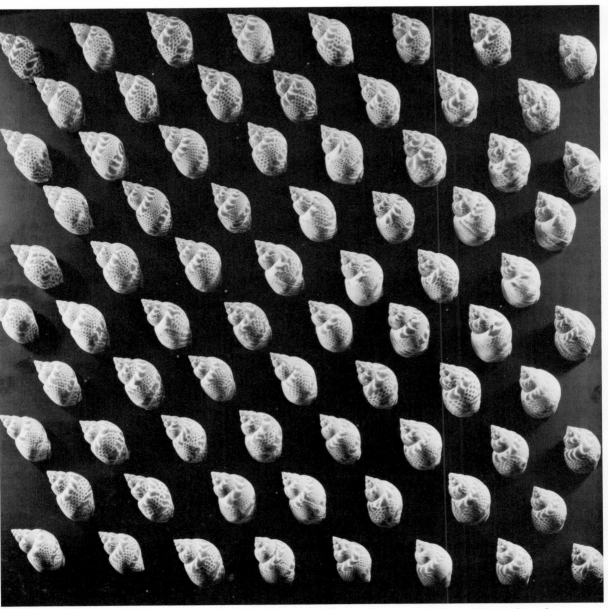

First paint a canvas board the color of your choice and then cover the entire canvas with shells (the same or different ones) in a geometric pattern. Use Elmer's glue or epoxy depending on the weight of the shells. These are Babylon (or Bai) shells. *Photo: Thomas Feist. Design: Jerome M. Eisenberg. Courtesy: The Collector's Cabinet, New York.*

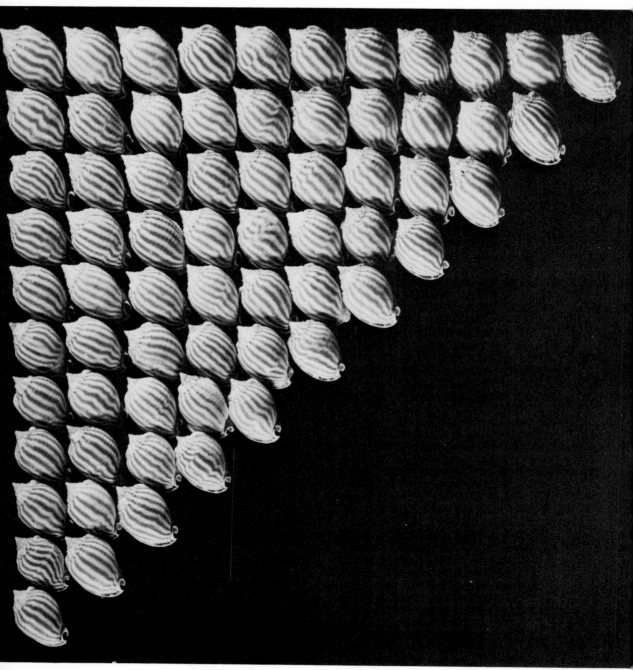

A very dramatic effect is obtained by making a geometric design in just one area of a very richly colored canvas. These shells are striped bonnets. *Photo: Thomas Feist. Design: Jerome M. Eisenberg. Courtesy: The Collector's Cabinet, New York.*

Shadow Boxes

Instead of putting your collage or picture into a simple frame, you can create a collage or sea scene in depth by making it in the form of a shadow box.

Shadow boxes are quite decorative and often add a bit of distinction to a wall grouping.

In making a shadow box with shells you will find you have a great deal more freedom in creating, as its three-dimensional aspect gives you more room to explore.

MATERIALS

Here as in the shell pictures is a good place to use all the odd and broken shells you have as well as other related materials, such as sea glass, glass fishing-net balls, various sea plants, driftwood, coral, stones smoothed by the surf, and so on.

An assortment of sea-related items to use in a shadow box.

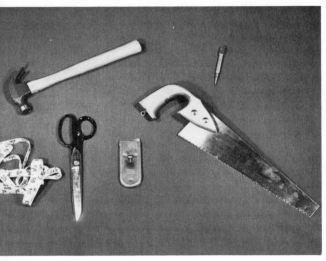

Tools needed to make a shadow box itself are: Tape measure, scissors or single-edge razor, saw, hammer, and center punch. Not pictured but also needed are epoxy and Elmer's glue. Krylon spray is optional.

The materials needed to make the shadow box and backing are: Four pieces of wood to make the frame. The width we recommend is 3 inches, and the thickness ½ inch. The box we will make is 19 x 14 inches, so we use two pieces of wood 19 inches long and two pieces 13 inches long. The backing is ¼-inch plywood 19 x 14 inches. Two pieces of track molding, one ½ inch wide and one ¼ inch wide. Finishing nails (1¼ inch and ½ inch), wood putty sticks, and sandpaper (coarse and fine). Also needed are wood stain or paint, a covering for the background (velour, wallpaper, contact paper, etc.) and a piece of glass to fit into the track molding and cover the picture.

When you go to the lumberyard to buy the wood, ask about any scrap pieces of hardwood—mahogany, oak, pine, etc.—they might have. You will get a better price on these scraps and they will suit the purpose perfectly. Most lumberyards will cut the wood you buy to your specifications free of charge. (The above wood, including the plywood backing, cost us under two dollars.)

First start three 1¼-inch finishing nails into one end of a 19-inch piece of wood, until they just show through the other side.

Then butt that piece into one of the 13-inch sides. Continue until all four corners are made.

With the punch, recess the nails a little into the wood.

Then sand the edges and corners with the coarse sandpaper.

Fill in all nail holes and joints with the wood putty stick, which you heat and use like a candle dripping.

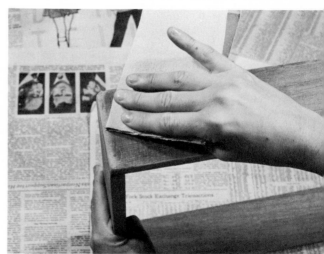

Then finish sanding with the fine-grain sandpaper for a smoothly finished box. Wipe down with a damp rag.

Here are the two pieces of track molding that will hold the glass. The wider piece (½ inch) is for the top of the frame and the ¼-inch piece is for the bottom.

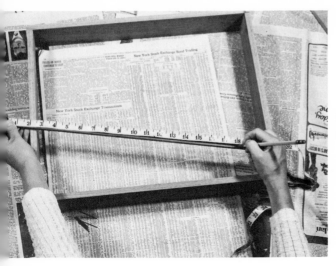

Cut the track molding to fit the inner edge of the frame.

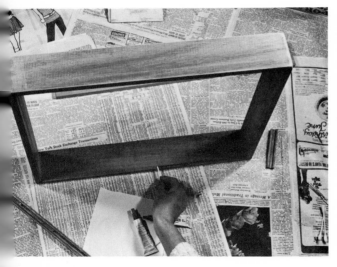

Epoxy the edge of the frame where the molding is to sit. This step is just for extra support.

Then lay the molding over the epoxy with the shorter finishing nails (½ inch) just started through the molding.

Hammer the nails in all the way. You probably will need the punch to do this as the groove in the molding is too narrow for a hammer head. Repeat the same process for the top molding.

Stain or paint the frame to your taste.

Sand down the edges of your plywood piece before covering it with the background material.

Here we are cutting a piece of blue fabric to cover the plywood and fold over about an inch all around.

We are stapling down one side . . .

and then flipping the plywood over and epoxying that edge . . .

then flipping it back to staple the top edge, and then repeating the epoxying process to get a very tight-fitting covering.

Now we are making sure we have no air pockets or wrinkles in the material before we staple the last side of the back.

Here is the completed covered plywood being set onto the frame.

Nail the plywood securely onto the shadow box frame.

There are other ways to cover the plywood backing as we mentioned earlier: wallpaper, contact paper, etc. Or you could paint it. Before you go out and buy a background covering for the picture, look around the house. Perhaps you will find some material that excites you as an interesting background, and might determine the direction you go with the picture itself.

Another interesting method would be to cover the plywood with sand or tiny pebbles (the kind that are used in fish tanks). Simply cover the plywood with a light coating of Elmer's glue and then sprinkle the sand or pebbles over the entire area. Fill in all vacant areas so that no wood shows through. Allow to dry at least an hour before continuing with the picture.

Designing the Sea Scene

Now that you are ready to begin, there are really no rules. Your imagination is your only guideline. You can make an abstract design, you can copy a scene from a picture, or one you have seen while diving, or you can simply create as you go along.

Using this picture of underwater life as a jumping-off point, we begin to lay out the shadow box design.

For this picture we are using various types of soft coral (sea fans), some sea-horses, shells, and a starfish.

We start by gluing on the various pieces of soft coral and sea fans in the areas we have decided.

Hold down the edges of the coral branches till they adhere to the backing.

Then we add the seahorses as though they were swimming around the sea fans.

Then a beautiful sundial shell, and also a starfish, which we adhere with the Devcon "5 Minute" Epoxy because it is heavy.

We also use the epoxy with this scorpion conch shell, and some additional shells climbing up the frame of the shadow box.

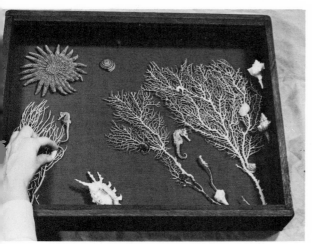

We add some small shells to the pieces of coral as though they were caught or feeding. And especially a flamingo tongue shell that we discussed in Chapter 1, as it lives on this soft coral.

To further accentuate the three-dimensional quality, we add some hard coral and assorted shells to the bottom of the frame, making sure the glass has room to slip into the track.

Fit the glass into the top wider track first, and let the glass slide into the bottom track which holds it in place.

Add eye hooks and picture wire to the back and the shadow box is ready for hanging.

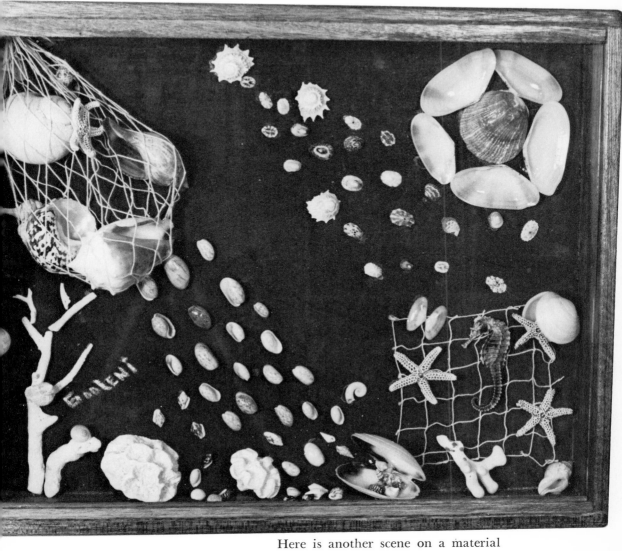

Here is another scene on a material backing. This one employs fish netting along with shells, coral, a seahorse, and several small starfish.

This shadow box is less abstract and more like the shell picture in the previous section. The background is a piece of ¼ inch plywood covered with a bamboo-textured piece of wallpaper. As you can see, the center of the flower is a starfish, the petals are various shells, and the stem is made up of razor clams. The sea garden effect is furthered with the use of various pieces of coral and a sea fan scattered around as if they were bushes. In the upper left-hand corner is a jawbone of a fish and two ark shells to represent a bee flying to the flower.

A shadow box in a wall display with
other shell pieces.

There are hundreds of other ways to use shells and it would be impossible to list them all. However, we would like to show you a few intriguing uses and then let you enjoy finding others on your own.

Here are various shells turned into jewel-like decorations by covering them with a gold-leaf paint. *Photo: Thomas Feist. Courtesy: Jerome M. Eisenberg, The Collector's Cabinet, New York.*

Matchbox

A simple matchbox, which can be purchased for pennies, can be decorated with shells to look like an interesting showpiece.

Measure the underside of the matchbox and cut a piece of felt or sponge to fit. Spread a thin amount of Elmer's glue over the bottom and attach the felt or sponge to it. After that dries, apply a thin coat of glue to the top of the box and sprinkle a coat of sand over it, filling in all the spaces. When that dries completely, apply a few shells or coral, with more glue, in an interesting design.

Picture Frames

Yet another idea is to decorate a simple picture frame with shells.

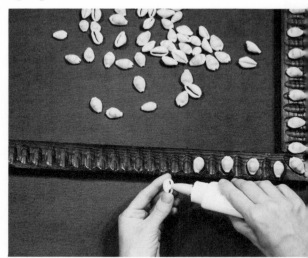

Here is a notched frame that we have started to dress up a bit with little yellow money cowries at fixed intervals around the frame.

Here is the completed frame ready for a picture or mirror.

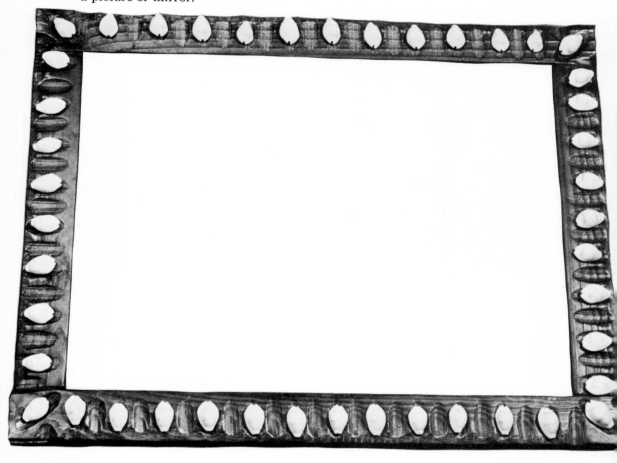

You could also cover an entire frame with shells.

Working a section at a time, spread on an even coat of adherent—Elmer's glue or epoxy, depending on the weight of the shells. Then place the shells, mixing colors and shapes as you prefer. Continue this way around the entire frame. There is no need to wait until the previous section dries. After the frame dries, you can spray the shells with the clear Krylon or you can spray on a color—silver or gilt or one of the colors in the picture to be framed.

Figurines

You have probably seen figurines such as these made from shells. Perhaps you want to try your hand at creating some figurines on your own.

The materials needed for a simple shell figure are few. You'll need "5 Minute" Epoxy (or Elmer's Glue-All). The epoxy is preferred in this instance as it will dry much more quickly and allow you to go on to the next step almost immediately. You'll need paint or magic marker to paint in the face or other markings you might wish to make. And of course shells. A bivalve is especially good for the base of any figure you do. Limpets are excellent for skirts and collars. Augers, miters, ceriths, olives, and the like are excellent for arms and legs. Once you begin you will find all kinds of imaginative ways to use the different shape shells.

Here we are using a clam shell for the base and a king's crown shell on which the figure is going to sit. The first step is to mix the epoxy.

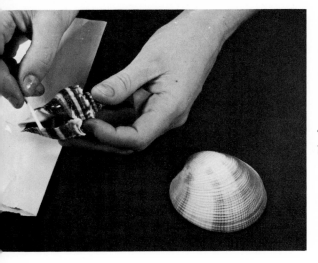

Then epoxy the king's crown to the base shell.

And set it firmly in place.

Here we are fitting two shells together for the upper legs and thighs. As you can see we have already picked out the shells to be used for the legs and feet.

The thighs are epoxied onto the seat. The rest of the figure will be built out from these two shells.

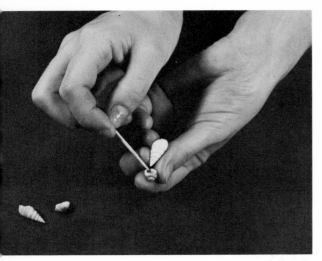

And now the feet are epoxied to the leg shells.

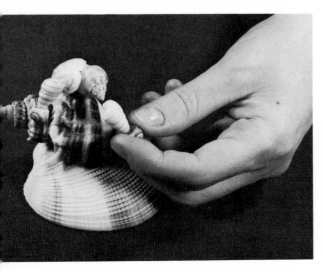

After they both dry, the legs are attached to the thigh shells in a natural angle for sitting.

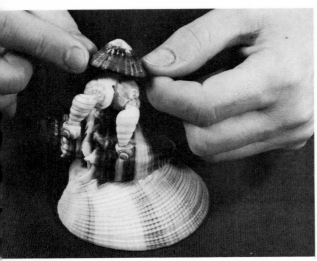

A limpet shell makes an excellent base for the next part of the body and looks like an outfit on the figure.

The trunk of the body is added next. This particular shell is a banded tree snail. It has a broken tip, which helps it fit flat against the limpet.

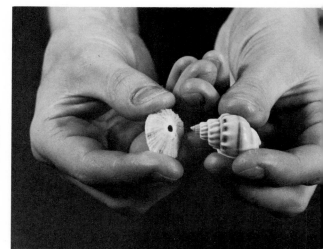

Another way to make a secure fit is to use a keyhole limpet which has a natural hole in it and fit a pointed shell into that hole to act as the body.

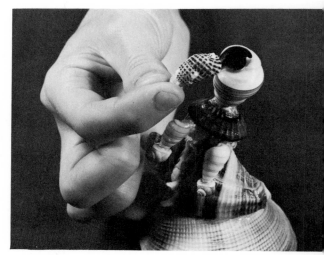

After the body is epoxied onto the limpet, the first arm shell is fitted into place.

Then fit the other arm next to it.

And cover them with another limpet to act as the shoulders or collar of the outfit.

You can add the lower arm or hands at this point.

The easiest way to make a face is to set a small clam shell at an angle into a slightly larger clam shell (which becomes the hat).

When these two shells are firmly epoxied together, set them on top of the shoulders.

Paint in the features and hair if you wish.

After reinforcing all joints with epoxy, spray the figure with clear Krylon to bring out the natural colors of the shells.

Here is the completed figure.

There are many variations, simpler and more complex, that you might try. Here, as in the other areas we explore, the possibilities are as endless as your imagination.

We would just like to show you one other way of approaching the figurines. In this method you build with shells out from a frame of another material. In this case we are using pipe cleaners.

Materials: Epoxy or Elmer's glue, toothpicks, and Q-Tip swabs, a hole punch or heavy screw (or hobbyist drill), and pipe cleaners.

Start twisting two pipe cleaners together from the center upward.

Continue until you have just enough for arms. Then bend them outward.

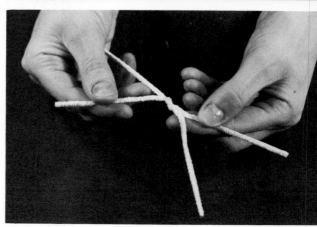

Make two holes in the base shell with a large screw or hole punch (depending on thickness of shell), or hobbyist drill if you have one. Here we are using a *Pecten swifti* for the base.

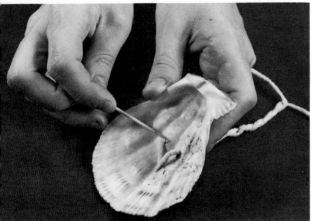

Fit the bottom tips of the pipe cleaners through the holes in the base and bend them. Then epoxy them securely to the shell (underside and topside as well).

Start the figure by fitting a shell (perhaps a cone) onto the middle section of the pipe cleaner. Epoxy it securely. Also bend the pipe cleaner legs outward a bit, as they are going to be the framework for a hoop skirt effect.

Start the skirt by matching two small clam shells and epoxying them to the base and the pipe cleaners. These two shells are the beginning of a layered skirt.

Place two small shells, for the tips of the shoes, where they might be peeking out from the skirt.

Then fit the front of the skirt over the shoes and against the two side clam shells. Do the same in the back. Continue the layered effect with two more side shells slightly higher up the pipe cleaners.

Continue with a front and back shell on this second level and then two more side shells, repeating the layering process until you reach the coned body.

Cut the pipe cleaner arms to fit into or against your arm shells. Epoxy them on, making sure they rest against the cone body as well, for additional support.

Add a flat shell for the shoulders or collar and also add the hands. Here we are placing a staff in her hand for an added touch.

The head is made the same way as before, using two clam shells.

After you paint in the face, reinforce
all joints, and spray with clear Krylon,
the figure is completed.

Jewel Box

A plain jewel box can be treated the same way as the picture frame. Just coat the top of the box with adherent and then arrange the shells in a pattern or picture, perhaps filling in all the spaces with grains of sand.

Here is that idea carried out over an entire box, using some exquisite large shells including a pearlized chambered nautilus and trochus shells, and some marble cones and large scallops.

This magnificent jewel box is from the Gloria Vanderbilt collection when it was shown at the Hallmark Gallery in New York as part of an exhibition called "The Collectors." It was made in Mexico by a local craftsman.

This is a decorative hanging piece from the Philippines, similar to Chinese wind chimes. The top part is made of half of a coconut which has been polished. And the chimes are the spines of the stone sea urchin. These spines (unlike the black sea urchin) are thick and stonelike, usually chocolate brown, banded at the top and bottom with white. They can be used in many decorative ways, including lovely jewelry pieces. *Courtesy: Harry and Marion Zelenko.*

There is no end of what you can do with shells in both original works and by transforming other materials into beautiful objects of art through the use of shells.

Shell Sculptures **7**

*W*hen we first started diving for and collecting large shells, like conch, we looked for a way to display them a little differently than just placing them on the bookcase or windowsill.

One day, in a pet store, we found some chunks of petrified wood. This gave us the idea of mounting the shells on various pieces of these beautiful rocks.

Simple Pieces

Pet stores and some florists are a good source of petrified wood, limestone, shale, and other such minerals, as they are used in decorating fish tanks and in some floral arrangements. We found these chunks of rock rather inexpensive, and just perfect to use as bases for the shells we wanted to display. It is best to pick pieces that have one comparatively smooth or straight side as the bottom.

Petrified wood (wood that has turned to quartz) with a large conch shell epoxied on top of it. This is a simple yet attractive decoration for a bookshelf or desk.

To give your piece a professional finished look, and at the same time protect your furniture from scratch marks, we suggest that you buy some felt material in a yardgoods store to cover the bottom of the mineral base.

Outline the shape of the base on the piece of felt.

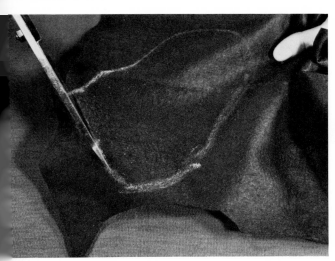

Cut along this outline, slightly smaller than indicated.

Cover the bottom of the mineral base with an adhesive, such as Elmer's Glue-All.

Place felt over glue.

Press into place and cut off any excess felt.

Shortly after this experiment with different mineral bases, we became fascinated by the pieces of driftwood we saw while beachcombing, and we began picking up interesting pieces along with the shells.

It was only a short step from there to combining our shells with the driftwood. First we used the pieces of driftwood as we found them, only washing and scrubbing them with a stiff brush to get the sand and dirt off.

Then we began to cut up the larger pieces we had found into various sizes to fit our needs, still trying to keep the natural line of the piece of wood.

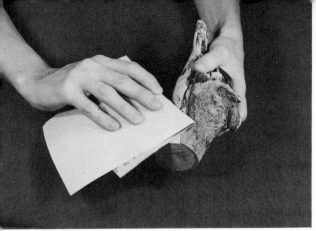

After cutting, sand various sections to give different texture effects to the piece.

Driftwood piece with Florida fighting conch.

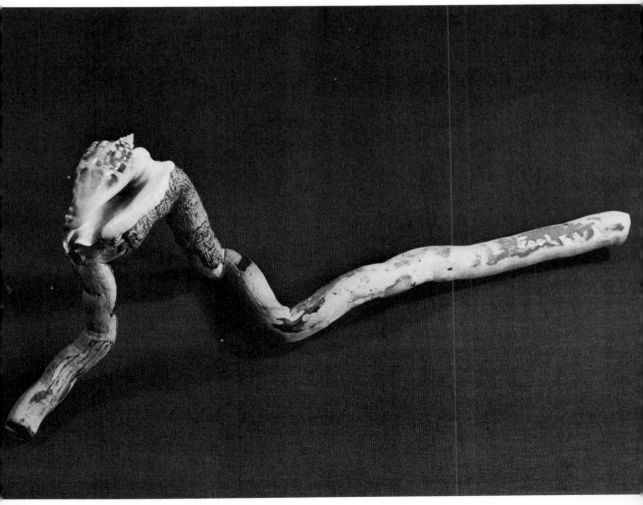

Free Forms

In order to give the pieces a firmer base, we found that the flat chunks of shale, sold in all aquarium supply stores, were just suited for this purpose.

Cover the bottom of the shale with felt as described before, and then epoxy the driftwood to the shale.

Then fit the shell onto the driftwood in the most interesting manner you can achieve. The design you create truly makes this a sculpture that is unique unto you.

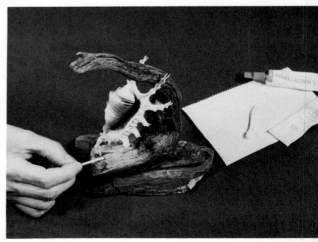

We suggest spraying the finished sculpture with the Krylon spray (clear) we use on all our pieces, in order to bring out the natural highlights of the shale, the driftwood, and the shell.

A scorpion conch shell from the Indo-Pacific on driftwood.

A ram's murex from the Indo-Pacific.

A fox shell from Florida.

From these simple pieces we gradually became more and more creative with our designs, and finally realized that we needed a better focus of attention in the form of a frame.

And the perfect frame we found was to place the sculpture in a clear acrylic box, commonly called Plexiglas.

Plexiglas Boxes as Frames
for Your Sculptures

We experimented with various sizes and color combinations (as Plexiglas comes in various shades other than clear), and found that for most of our purposes a box 6 x 6 x 7 would house almost any design we created. (When working in quantity, we found that by keeping the boxes uniform our cutting costs were kept down.) If you cut your own boxes, as we will illustrate later, you will not have this concern.

Also we found that the various shaded sides took away from the object within. Although in certain cases you might wish to use one or two panels of a different shade, for our purposes we prefer a clear acrylic for the five sides, and for the base piece a dark smoke color. This dark base highlights the sculpture and also helps hide any extra glue drippings. If you prefer, a completely clear cube gives a lighter, more airy feeling.

There are three ways to obtain the Plexiglas boxes you will need to frame your sculptures.

First, you can have them cut and made to order by a manufacturer (see Index of Supplies). When we have large orders to fill we use this procedure to save time.

If you do order your boxes this way, you should request five sides to be cemented and the sixth side (the base) to be separate, so that you can attach your sculpture to it. Then set the five-sided section over it and cement closed.

Second, you can save some money and also have the enjoyment of making the box yourself, by ordering the pieces cut to size and then cementing the sides together.

Using a solvent cement for acrylic sheets (available where you purchase the Plexiglas), cement the first two sides together.

Do the same for the third, fourth, and fifth sides. And then proceed as above with the base.

Third, for those of you who would like to make the box from scratch, we will at the end of this chapter describe that process in detail.

At this point, let us get back to the sculpture itself. For these sculptures, we begin the same way as for the free-form pieces, except that now we have a space limitation on our design.

Also, the bases we use for the shells must be absolutely flat or they will not adhere well to the Plexiglas. We were able to cut the driftwood pieces ourselves. But the mineral pieces require the services of a lapidary, especially the petrified wood bases, which can be cut only with a diamond saw.

Scrub the mineral or driftwood base.

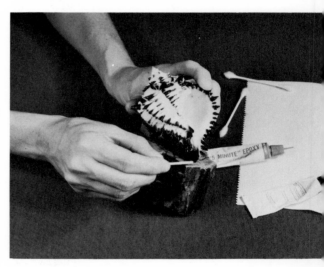

Set the shell on the base at the most attractive angle and epoxy it on.

Spray with the clear Krylon.

Then epoxy the base of the sculpture onto the Plexiglass base, or use an electric glue gun (available at a minimal price at most hardware stores) instead.

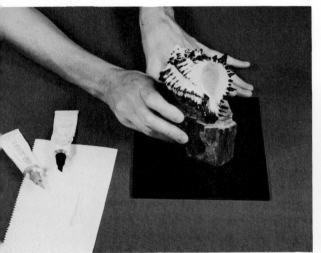

Set it at an interesting angle.

Before closing the box, spray the entire inside surface with an antistatic cleaner and polish it dry, making sure to remove all dirt smudges and lint. "Lemon" Pledge works equally as well.

Place the five-sided cube over the base and seal. This is a *Murex nigritus* on petrified wood.

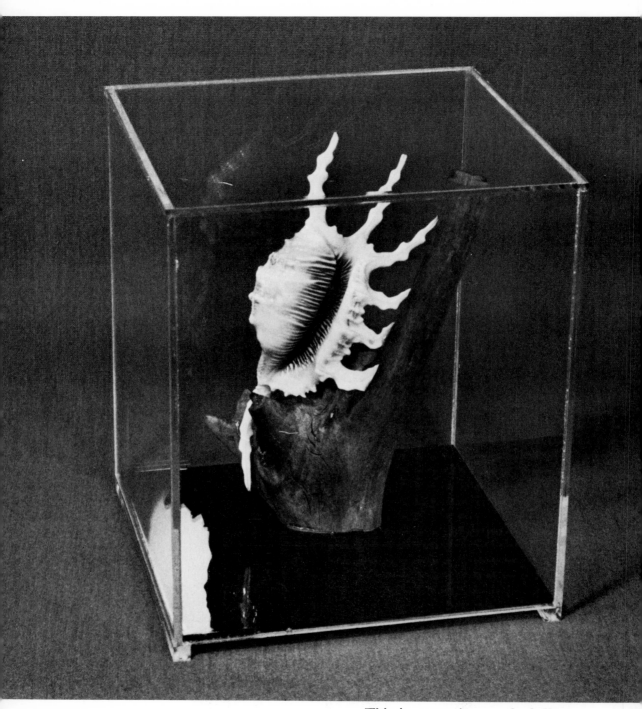

This is a scorpion conch shell on a
piece of driftwood.

This is a ram's murex on driftwood.

This is a pink-mouthed murex seated
on a strangely couch-like piece of
driftwood.

Another idea is to glue shells to the outside of a Plexiglas box in an interesting pattern with Elmer's glue. As Elmer's glue can be removed with soap and water, you can change the design anytime you wish. *Photo: Thomas Feist. Design: Jerome M. Eisenberg. Courtesy: Jerome M. Eisenberg, The Collector's Cabinet, New York.*

Now for those of you interested in purchasing the Plexiglas in sheets and cutting your own boxes, The Rohm and Haas Company, manufacturers of Plexiglas, has provided us with detailed pictures and instructions. (See the Index of Supplies for where to send for the various booklets they have available.)

Working with Plexiglas can be fascinating and fun. You can cut it with standard power tools or by hand, and then solvent-cement it to produce strong, transparent joints.

Plexiglas is a rigid, resilient, acrylic plastic sheet material, which can be purchased nationwide through building supply dealers, some hardware stores, glass and plastic outlets, and some paint stores. It is available in many sizes, colors, and thicknesses.

There are several methods of cutting Plexiglas to size, depending on the tools you have available.

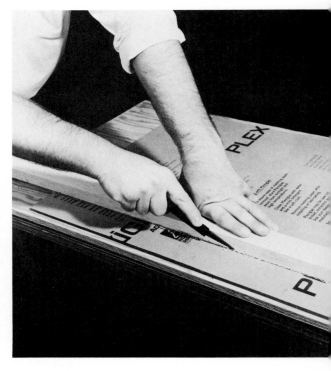

SCRIBING AND BREAKING PLEXIGLAS* WITH A SPECIAL CUTTING TOOL: Using a straight-edge as a guide, place the point of the Plexiglas acrylic sheet cutting tool at the edge of the material and, applying firm pressure, draw the cutting point the full width of the material. Keep masking paper on Plexiglas during this and the breaking procedures.

* Plexiglas is a registered trademark of Rohm and Haas Company, Reg. U.S. Pat. Off.

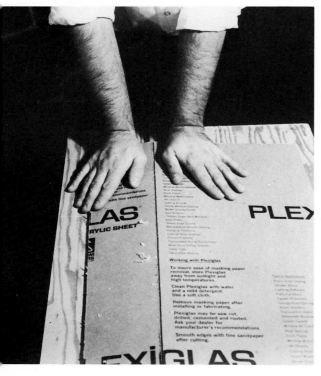

BREAKING: To break, the scribed line should be positioned face up over a ¾-inch diameter wood dowel running the length of the intended break. Hold the sheet with one hand and apply downward pressure on the short side of the break with the other. The hands should be kept adjacent to one another and successively repositioned about 2 inches in back of the break as it progresses along the scribed line. The minimum cut-off width is about 1½ inches.

SAWING

Circular saws are ideal for straight cutting of Plexiglas. Use a steel cross-cut blade which is recommended for finish cuts on plywood, veneers, laminates, etc. The blade should have at least 6 teeth per inch. All the teeth should be of the same shape, height, and point to point distance. Set the blade height just a little above the thickness of the sheet to prevent chipping. Hold Plexiglas down firmly when cutting—do not force-feed.

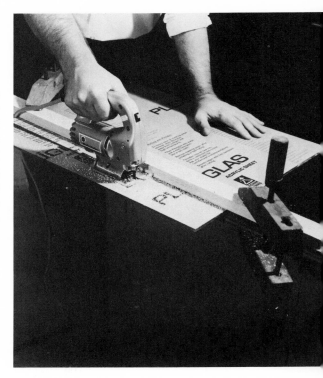

Saber, band, and reciprocating jigsaws will easily cut curved shapes. Saber and reciprocating jigsaw blades should have at least 14 teeth per inch. Straight cuts can be made with a saber or hand jigsaw by guiding the tool along a straight edge. Band saws should have at least 10 teeth per inch. Hold Plexiglas down firmly when cutting—do not force-feed.

FINISHING

Sanding the sawed edges: Sawed edges and other tool marks should be removed from Plexiglas by scraping the edges smooth with a sharp knife or by sanding with medium grit (60–80) paper. This will increase the breakage resistance of the Plexiglas. **To further improve the appearance of the surface or edge, follow this with "wet or dry"** (150) grit sandpaper.

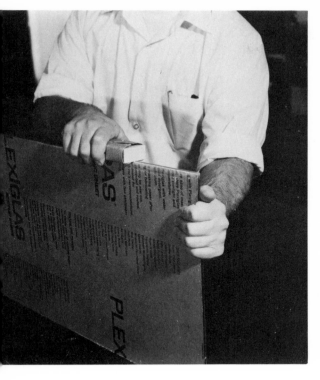

Buffing the edges smooth: For a transparent Plexiglas edge, follow 60–80 grit sanding and "wet or dry" 150 grit sanding with grits to 400 and buff with a clean muslin wheel dressed with a good grade of fine grit buffing compound. Finish up with a clean soft cotton-flannel wheel.

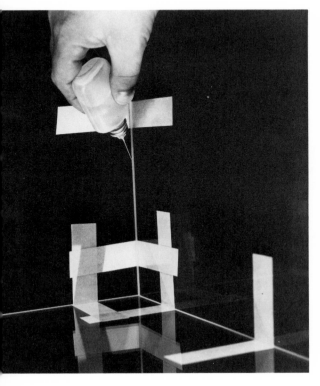

Solvent-cementing the sides together: Capillary-cementing Plexiglas with a solvent (methylene chloride "MDC," ethylene dichloride "EDC," or 1–1–2 trichlorethane) is an easy method of joining two pieces of Plexiglas. Remove protective masking paper. Sand surfaces to be cemented; do not polish. Apply solvent to joint with the Plexiglas acrylic sheet solvent applicator for cementing, a syringe, oilcan with a very fine spout, eyedropper, or small paintbrush; let joint dry thoroughly.

To make a box 6 x 6 x 7 inches, the size we find most useful, start by cutting four pieces of ¼-inch-thick Plexiglas 6½ inches in height, and 5¾ inches wide for the sides.

Then cut two pieces 6 x 6 inches for the top and base. (Remember our suggestion of using a dark smoke color for the base piece.)

If you use ⅛-inch Plexiglas instead of ¼-inch, you must recalculate your sizes using eighths rather than quarters.

These shell sculptures in Plexiglas boxes will be the highlight of your living room or anywhere that you decide to display them.

You can keep them beautiful and dust free by periodically spraying them with an antistatic cleaner (such as listed in Index of Supplies) or "Lemon" Pledge; or with a good grade of automobile paste wax (not a cleaner-wax combination). Apply a thin even coat and wipe off and buff lightly with a clean cotton flannel or jersey cloth. After polishing, wipe with a clean damp cloth to ground any electrostatic charges that may attract dust particles.

Shell Collections 8

"Why a person decides to collect is as varied as the people are themselves. Historical preservation can be the reason, or beauty, uniqueness, nostalgia, investment, infatuation, or simply a form of momentary madness. Collecting is a human characteristic which goes back to prehistoric times. Throughout history collecting has increased during periods of affluence and relative calm." *

Throughout the world there are many shell collections. Some are individually owned and others are housed in museums.

Most museums of natural history have an extensive shell collection. Practically every major city has a museum of natural history and most of them have no admission charge. You probably won't be able to see their whole collection as the majority of their shells are catalogued and tucked away in drawers. But you probably will be able to see a beautiful selection on display for the general public. You will be able to see most of the different species from the various provinces of the world of shells. But there are some rare species that are on view perhaps at only one museum. For example, the museum in Wales has a *Conus Duravelli* that until recently was the only known specimen of this cone shell. This museum in Wales, whose curator is S. Peter Dance, one of the leading malacologists and author of many fine books on shells, has one of the finest shell collections of any museum in the world.

The Philadelphia Museum and the New York Museum of National History have extensive and prized collections also. See the listing of additional museum collections at the end of the book.

One of the finest and most extensive individual collections is owned by Simon De Marco in Fort Myers, Florida. There is also an excellent private collection owned by a man named Pancho, housed in the back of his shell store Shellorama in Fort Lauderdale, Florida. (See Index of Supplies and the listing of museums.) Both these collections are on display to the public at no charge. Also there is a similar display in a shell store on Sanibel Island, Florida, owned by Mrs. Denny.

As we stated before, shell collecting is becoming more and more popular to a growing number of people around the world. And from the beginner to the avid conchologist, the search for those special "rare shells" continues.

We have listed in the Bibliography several books and organizations that specialize in setting prices on various shells. Remember prices vary with supply (the rarity of the shell) and demand (just how much a particular collector wants a certain shell).

Another factor in determining the price a shell will bring is the condition the shell is in (or its "grade").

---

* Introduction from the exhibition "The Collectors," Hallmark Gallery, New York.

A "first grade" shell is one usually collected in its natural habitat with the animal still alive. If this shell is a univalve, you would need to save the operculum ("trap door") along with the shell.* If it is a bivalve, you would need both shells preferably still hinged together. A "first grade" shell is as perfect as possible for that species, remembering, of course, there is nothing truly perfect in nature. Cowries are the easiest to obtain in first grade condition.

A "second grade" shell is one that perhaps has a noticeable growth mark or is a little chipped, etc. It usually costs much less than a first grade shell. If you are buying shells for jewelry or artwork or collecting, either of these grades is perfect for your uses. Any lower grade would have bad discolorations or breakage and perhaps only be useful in collage work as you have seen in the chapter on collage.

If your collection is to be a formal scientific type you must keep a record of the actual locale in which the shell was found, the date, how obtained (dredging, diving, etc.), in what type of area, and the genus and species name. For example:

Cypraea zebra Linne (measled cowrie)
August 19, 1972
Dog Island, approx. 5 miles off Virgin Gorda, British Virgin Islands
Skin diving, found under a coral head

If you buy your shells from other collectors they will give you this information, as will most of the shell stores from which you might buy. If you find the shell yourself, remember to make note of all the pertinent information.

A selection of shells with their locality data, as displayed in The Collector's Cabinet, a shell store in New York.

Of course it is possible to collect shells in a less formal manner. You may want to collect for your own enjoyment a sampling of the various species of shells around the world (or from a specific area) without regard to the formal identifications. You may wish to collect only the shells you find yourself, you may wish to buy your shells, or you may wish a combination of the two.

* Some species of univalves have no operculum.

A sampling of shells that would make a good beginning for a collection. These shells are classic representatives of the Indo-Pacific Province. They can probably be purchased from a good shell store as a unit or individually. The entire selection would cost around $20. Each shell will usually have a card with its identification and locality data. *Photo: Thomas Feist. Courtesy: Jerome M. Eisenberg, The Collector's Cabinet, New York.*

This grouping of some less common shells to spice up your collection ranges in price from $2.50 to $5 each. This selection would run about $20. It includes the purple and orange pecten and the *Voluta imperialis*. *Photo: Thomas Feist. Courtesy: Jerome M. Eisenberg, The Collector's Cabinet, New York.*

This grouping includes some collector's delights and would run about $50. Included are the exotic *Tibia fusus* and the precious wentletrap. *Photo: Thomas Feist. Courtesy: The Collector's Cabinet, New York.*

The question now arises as to the way you may want to display your collection. You can choose from a formal display case or drawer case all the way down to a shoe box in the closet. In between these extremes is a whole range of exciting and interesting possibilities. We would like to show you a few ways and perhaps encourage you to explore even more interesting ways using your shells as inspiration.

Here are some rather informal shell displays. An oversized brandy snifter is a very useful shell holder, as is this apothecary jar full of beautifully colored tiny shells gathered along the beaches of the Caribbean.

Another way is to display your shells in a way that is decorative as well as useful.

We made a beautiful coffee table from an old wine barrel in which to display some of our shells.

First we had the barrel cut in half and a false bottom added at about the midway point. Then we stained and polished it and added three screw-in legs.

We measured and cut a piece of blue velour to fit the false bottom. This gave the barrel a rather elegant yet warm feeling. We added four L brackets on which to rest the glass top, and covered these brackets with blue velour also.

On the velour, we arranged our most prized shells and coral that we had gathered from our various diving trips around the world.

When we put the last cowrie on the tip of a piece of staghorn coral, we knew our coffee table was finished. Then we measured the inner diameter of the top and had a glazier cut a 1/4-inch-thick piece of glass to just fit inside the barrel top.

This coffee table sits in a place of honor in front of our sofa. Several people have offered to buy it, and some have suggested that we go into production with it. But it is our pride and joy, second only to our daughter, Julie

Harry and Marion Zelenko, internationally known designers, and their family are also shell collectors. Here is a simple yet exquisite coffee table they designed and executed to house and display part of their collection. It is made of rosewood with a recessed glass top and sits in the center of their living room.

Another version made of burl wood
houses some more of their collection
and is placed in the Zelenko's foyer
area.

Another way to display shells is to make them into decorative pieces, such as we showed in the chapter on shell pictures and collages.

Sometimes people make a collection of these objects made from shells. Mr. and Mrs. Wyatt Cooper (Gloria Vanderbilt) have such a collection. Their love of shells has led them to assemble beautiful shell objects made by craftsmen throughout the world.

Here is part of their shell collection on display at the Hallmark Gallery, New York, as part of an exhibition called "The Collectors," held in the summer of 1971.

And last, an example of nature's very own collector. This is a Japanese carrier shell that attaches empty shells to itself, many times in very interesting patterns.

Shells can be collected in many ways and for many reasons. Once you begin you will see in what direction your interests will lead you.

We hope this book has expanded your knowledge and appreciation of shells and has given you the means to fulfill this new-found knowledge and appreciation of the shell in a creative way.

Down by the sea I came to see
What the vast ocean would bring to me.
Would it be a gift of love
Or a treasure rare
Or just the wind above.
But to my surprise I found a shell
And I called it sunrise.

Gooleni, 1972

GLOSSARY

Bits and Burrs—Rough-headed pieces used for drilling.

Bivalves (Pelecypods)—Mollusks with two shells (valves) hinged together.

Conchology—The study and collecting of shells. (Conchologist.)

Findings—The various parts of jewelry needed to make the whole, including jump rings, bell caps, hooks, chains, etc.

Gastropods—*see* Univalves.

Malacology—The scientific study of mollusks. (Malacologist.)

Mantle—The enveloping membrane of a shell.

Mollusk—The phylum of invertebrates usually protected by a calcareous shell.

Operculum—The calcareous plate attached to the bottom of the foot of the univalve.

Pelecypods—*see* Bivalves.

Periostracum—The outer coating of the shell, sometimes shiny, rough, furry, or fibrous.

Scuba—Self-Contained Underwater Breathing Apparatus.

Univalves—Single-shelled mollusks, usually spiral-shaped in form.

Museums, Aquariums, and Other Shell Exhibits

United States National Museum, part of the Smithsonian Institution, Washington, D.C.
American Museum of Natural History, New York, New York
Philadelphia Museum of Natural History, Philadelphia, Pennsylvania
Carnegie Museum, Pittsburgh, Pennsylvania
Field Museum of Natural History, Chicago, Illinois
Museum of Zoology, University of Michigan, Ann Arbor, Michigan
Los Angeles County Museum, Los Angeles, California
Oakland Museum, Oakland, California
Santa Barbara Museum of Natural History, Santa Barbara, California
Washington State Museum, Olympia, Washington
Bernice P. Bishop Museum, Honolulu, Hawaii
Seaquarium, Key Biscayne, Florida
The Steinhart Aquarium, San Francisco, California
Pancho's Shellorama, North Federal Highway, Dania, Florida
Sanibel Island Exhibit, Sanibel Island, Florida
Simon De Marco Museum, Fort Myers, Florida

BIBLIOGRAPHY

Books on Shell Identification:

ABBOTT, R. TUCKER. *American Seashells.* Princeton, N.J.: D. Van Nostrand Co., Inc., 1954.
———. *Kingdom of the Seashell.* New York: Crown Publishers, Inc.
———. *Sea Shells of the World.* New York: Golden Press, 1962.
ALLAN, J. *Australian Shells.* Melbourne: Georgian House.
KIRA, T. *Shells of the Western Pacific in Color.* Osaka, Japan: Hoikusha.
STIX, HUGH AND MARGUERITE, ABBOTT, RITA. *The Shell: Four Hundred Million Years of Inspired Design.* New York: Harry N. Abrams, Inc.
WARMKE, G. L., AND ABBOTT, R. T. *Caribbean Seashells.* Narbeth, Pa.: Livingston Publishing Co.

A list of selected books on shell identification is available from the Division of Mollusks, United States National Museum, Smithsonian Institution, Washington, D.C. 20560.

See also the Index of Supplies, under Shell Sources, for illustrated booklets of shell identification.

Books on Collecting Shells:

ABBOTT, R. T. *How to Collect Shells.* Write to American Malacological Union (Box 318, Route 2), Marinette, Wis. 54143.
DANCE, S. PETER. *Shell Collecting.* London: Farber & Farber; Berkeley: University of California Press.

Books on Trading Shells and Evaluating Their Worth:

PRATT, RICHARD E. *Directory of Conchologists.* (P.O. Box 133, Ocean Drive Beach, S.C. 29582).
WAGNER, ROBERT J. L., AND ABBOTT, R. TUCKER. *Van Nostrand's Standard Catalogue of Shells.* Princeton, N.J.: D. Van Nostrand Co., Inc., 1964.

Books on Underwater Life:

COSTEAU, JACQUES-YVES, AND DUGAN, JAMES. *The Living Sea.* New York: Harper & Row, 1963.
NATIONAL GEOGRAPHIC SOCIETY. *World Beneath the Sea.* Washington, D.C.: National Geographic Society.
SLOSKY AND WALKER. *Guide to the Underwater.* New York: Sterling Publishing Co., Inc.

A $7.50 yearly subscription to the National Oceanographic Society, 10 Rickenbacker Causeway, Virginia Key, Miami, Florida, includes two bimonthly publications, *Sea Frontiers* and *Sea Secrets.* They are very informative magazines about scientific study and exploration of the ocean and mollusks. The subscription is tax deductible.

Books on Shells in General:

JOHNS, V. P. *She Sells Seashells.* New York: Funk & Wagnalls.
LINDBERGH, ANNE MORROW. *Gift from the Sea.* New York: Pantheon, 1955. Paperback edition, Signet.

Collages:

VANDERBILT, GLORIA. *Book of Collages.* Princeton, N.J.: D. Van Nostrand Co., Inc.

INDEX OF SUPPLIES

Shells

Walbead, Inc.
38 West 37 Street
New York, New York 10018
Shells and jewelry findings prepackaged. Available at hobby and craft outlets. Also seashell jewelry in kit form.

* Seashells Unlimited
590 Third Avenue
New York, New York 10016
LE 2-8690
No mail orders. Excellent selection of shells and coral.

The Collector's Cabinet
1000 Madison Avenue
New York, New York 10028
Also in Boston, Mass.
Illustrated booklet, "A Collector's Guide to Sea Shells," is $1.00, refundable with first purchase of shells. Excellent selection of shells, coral, and minerals. Price list available. Mail orders.

Gooleni
11 Riverside Drive
Suite 5 VE
New York, New York 10023
All shells and jewelry findings. Large and small orders. Prices on request. Mail orders.

Benjane Arts
777 Hempstead Turnpike
Franklin Square, New York 11010
Illustrated catalogue and price list available on request. Mail orders.

* Astro Minerals Limited
155 East 34th Street
New York, N.Y. 10016

The Shell Factory
P.O. Box BB
Fort Myers, Florida
Illustrated color catalogue and price list available on request. Mail orders. First order—$100.00 minimum.

Pancho's Shellorama
1450 North Federal Highway
Dania, Florida (near Fort Lauderdale)
No mail orders. No catalogue. Very large selection of shells

40 Fathoms Shell Divers
1922 North Federal Highway
Dania, Florida
No catalogue. Very large selection of shells

Diamonds
Coral Gables, Florida
No catalogue. Very large selection of shells

Ferguson's Marine Specialties
617 North Fries Avenue
Wilmington, California 90744
Mostly Mexican shells. No catalogue.

Benson Co.
220 East Pacific Coast Highway
Long Beach, California 90806
Catalague available. Corals and shells.

* The Shell Shed
122 Agate Avenue
Balboa Island, California 92662
No catalogue.

The Blue Mussel
475 Fifth Avenue South
Naples, Florida 33940

Petrified wood, other minerals, and driftwood

Walker Minerals
805 Lexington Avenue
New York, New York 10021
All minerals sold and cut and polished.

Aquarium Stock
31 Warren Street
New York, New York 10013
Petrified wood, shale, other minerals.

* Retail only. All other listings sell both retail and wholesale.

Joseph's Driftwood
1430 North Federal Highway
Dania, Florida
Very large selection of driftwood.

*Also available at most pet shops,
aquarium supply stores, and many
florists.*

Jewelry findings

* Eastern Findings Corp.
19 West 34 Street
New York, New York 10001
*Catalogue on request. Minimum
orders: 25 feet of chain, 1 gross other
findings.*

Allcraft
22 West 48 Street
New York, New York 10036
*14-karat gold findings only. Also gold
wire—round, square, etc. Catalogue
on request.*

Magic Novelty Co.
95 Morton Street
New York, New York 10014
*Wholesale only. Large orders only.
Catalogue on request.*

Metal City Finding Corp.
450 West 31 Street
New York, New York 10001
*Minimum order: 1 gross of any item.
Catalogue on request.*

* Federal Chain Company
141 Georgia Avenue
Providence, Rhode Island
Branches: New York, Chicago,
Los Angeles
*Wholesale only. Catalogue available.
Large orders preferred. Chains only.*

House of Bargains
195 Seventh Avenue
New York, New York 10011
*No mail orders. A bargain-basement-
type store of jewelry findings.*

Gordon's
1850 East Pacific Coast Highway
Long Beach, California 90804
Catalogue available.

Western Trimmings Corp.
8575 W. Washington Blvd.
Culver City, California 90230
Catalogue available.

*Providence, Rhode Island, is the
center for jewelry findings and all the
major companies are based there.*

*Also look in your local Yellow
Pages under Jewelers' Supplies and
Findings for additional sources.*

*Don't be intimidated by minimum
orders of a gross or more. Many times
a gross of a certain finding will cost
you less from these sources than a
dozen of the same finding would cost
in a hobby store.*

Plexiglas

Rohm & Haas Co.
P.O. Box 9730
Philadelphia, Pennsylvania 19140
*For information, send 25 cents for "Do
It Yourself With Plexiglas Acrylic
Sheet" booklet, or pick one up at your
local dealer's. Other booklets on using
Plexiglas are also available. Also any
questions you may have will be an-
swered gladly.*

Plexiglas sheets

Industrial Plastics
324 Canal Street
New York, New York

Sam Flax Inc.
25 East 28 Street
New York, New York
And other locations.

Plastics Center
65 Fourth Avenue
New York, New York

Century Lumber Yard
1875 Second Avenue
New York, New York

* Note: The bars (1¾ and 1⅝ inches) we
use in the more complex neckpieces (Chapter
4) are available only at Federal Chain Company and Eastern.

Plexiglas boxes

Leo Morris
Modular Fabricators
199 N. 8 Street
Brooklyn, New York 11211
Plexiglas sheets and boxes made to any specification. Mail orders welcome. Prices on request.

Also available at other art supply stores, lumberyards, plastic supermarkets, or a local distributor in your area:

Solvents for cementing Plexiglas sheets

IPS Weldon-3
MDC Cement Solvent Type (Guard Polymer & Chemicals Inc.)
Also available—a fine-spout applicator for solvent cement, or a fine-point eyedropper.

Antistatic cleaners for Plexiglas

Lighting P-99 (Guard Coating & Chemicals, Kearney, New Jersey)
Brillianize (Kleenmaster Chemicals, Omaha, Nebraska)
Glazcote
Formula AR
Klear
"Lemon" Pledge

Drill and drill parts

Dremel Manufacturing Co.
Racine, Wisconsin
Mail orders, or available through local distributors.

Bits and Burrs:
Abe Bass, Inc.
220 East 23 Street
New York, New York 10010

Also any dental equipment and supply house and any good hobby store.

Adherents and Spray

Elmer's Glue, Borden Co., New York

Devcon "5 Minute" Epoxy
Clear, dries rapidly.

Epoxy 330 (Hughes Associates, Excelsior, Minnesota
Clear, hardens in two hours.

Thermogrip Electric Glue gun and glue kit, USM Corp., 221 Oley Street, Reading , Pennsylvania 19601

Krylon Crystal Clear acrylic spray, Borden Co., New York
Also available in assorted colors for other effects.

INDEX

Page numbers in *italics* indicate an illustration.